G000075369

# THE MARTIANS ARE COMING!

# THE MARTIANS ARE COMING!

## THE TRUE STORY OF ORSON WELLES' 1938 PANIC BROADCAST

ALAN GALLOP

AMBERLEY

*This book is dedicated to my friend, Ray Berry*
*1930–2010*

First published 2011

Amberley Publishing
The Hill, Stroud
Gloucestershire GL5 4EP

www.amberleybooks.com

Copyright © Alan Gallop 2011

The right of Alan Gallop to be identified as the Author
of this work has been asserted in accordance with the
Copyrights, Designs and Patents Act 1988.

British Library Cataloguing in Publication Data.
A catalogue record for this book is available from the British Library.

ISBN 978-1-4456-0223-3

Typeset in 10pt on 12pt Sabon.
Typesetting and Origination by Amberley Publishing.
Printed in the UK.

# Contents

# Hoaxes and Close Encounters with Orson Welles

In March 2010, *Time* magazine ran an article about the most shocking hoaxes to have fooled the world. They included the case of Anna Anderson, a young girl fished out of a Berlin canal in 1920 who claimed to be Grand Duchess Anastasia Nikolaevna of Russia, the youngest daughter of Tsar Nicholas II. She was a fake, but for over thirty years she convinced hundreds of people that she was the real thing.

In 2009 the world watched in horror as authorities chased a runaway helium balloon believed to be carrying a six-year-old boy across the skies of northern Colorado. Horror turned to relief when it was revealed that the boy had failed to take flight and was hiding in his parent's attic. It was later learned that his father had concocted the flyaway child tale in a bid for reality TV stardom.

In 1983, the German magazine *Stern* carried an exclusive report claiming they had acquired 'the most explosive diaries in history' – the collected diaries of Adolf Hitler. A *Stern* journalist said the documents had been hidden away in East Germany after being recovered from a crashed aircraft in 1945. The magazine paid $6 million for the diaries, which passed three handwriting tests before being identified as 'grotesquely superficial fakes' produced on modern paper using 1980s-era ink and riddled with historical inaccuracies.

Other hoaxes included the story of a uniformed officer who arrived in Dover in 1814 with news that Napoleon Bonaparte was dead, meaning that England's war with the Bourbons was over. The value of government securities on the London Stock Exchange soared until it was found to be a hoax – it was another seven years before Napoleon died in exile on St Helena after his defeat at Waterloo.

When the first fragments of *Eoanthropus dawsoni* – better known as the Piltdown Man – were unearthed in East Sussex in 1912, scientists believed they had finally found definitive proof of mankind's evolution: the missing link between man and ape. Over the next forty years, more than 500 scientific essays were written on the fossil, but the discovery was proved to be a deliberate hoax in 1953. Piltdown Man turned out to be more of a patchwork man, his remains being an amalgamation of the lower jawbone of an orangutan and the skull of a fully developed human.

And then there was the story of how the young American actor Orson Welles and his legendary 1938 Halloween-eve radio broadcast of H. G. Wells' *The War of the Worlds* hoaxed America into believing that extraterrestrials had landed in New Jersey and were on a killing spree across the state. Millions had tuned in and a good percentage believed that what they heard was true. They evacuated their homes and ran amok through their neighbourhoods, screaming that everybody must flee for their lives.

Of all the famous hoaxes identified by *Time* magazine, *The War of the Worlds* was the only one that was unintentional. None of the actors taking part in the broadcast had any idea about the effect their play would have on an audience. After all, newspapers and radio listings magazines had advertised the programme in advance as part of a series of weekly plays by *The Mercury Theatre on the Air* that had been going on for nearly two months. But the show panicked America, which at the time was expecting to be plunged into another European war, taking the country back into the terrible depression that had brought the nation to its knees earlier in the decade.

Welles' *The War of the Worlds* production has become one of the most famous radio broadcasts in history. For many, it ranks alongside Chamberlain's 1939 declaration of war with Germany, Roosevelt's 1941 Infamy Speech the day after the attack on Pearl Harbour, and announcements of deaths of monarchs, presidents, and showbusiness and sporting personalities. They were all announced on the radio and heard by millions.

By the time Orson Welles and *The Mercury Theatre on the Air*'s actors stood in front of their microphones to unintentionally scare America's collective wits, radio had become the world's most powerful source of information. Radio had overtaken newspapers for delivery of up-to-the-minute news from across the globe. There was still a massive market for newspapers and magazines, but radio brought news, entertainment and information directly into people's homes, cars and workplaces. Radio was immediate and by 1938 it was not unusual for programmes to be interrupted by newsflash bulletins from correspondents reporting the latest news on everything from the Wall Street Crash to Nazi warmongering.

Thanks to *The War of the Worlds*, twenty-three-year-old wunderkind Orson Welles became a household name. The 'panic broadcast' was his ticket to Hollywood, where he was given carte blanche to write, produce, direct and star in almost any film he wanted to make. After one or two false starts, he directed a film now regarded by many to be one of the greatest ever made – *Citizen Kane*. But Welles' maverick methods upset producers and he made enemies of people who wanted him put in his place. After directing two films for RKO (*Citizen Kane* and *The Magnificent Ambersons*) and being told to abandon a third (*It's All True*), the freedom he had briefly enjoyed in Hollywood was taken away for good.

This book allows readers to step inside H. G. Wells' time machine and travel back to New York in 1938. But it is not only about events surrounding the making of a single hour-long radio play broadcast in America over seventy years ago, it is also about America – and Americans – at the time the broadcast went on air. It is about Welles' career before he became the best-known voice on American radio, the people he worked with, and his achievements as an actor and director in the theatre and on radio.

* * *

I had three personal close encounters with Orson Welles. Between 1966 and 1978 I worked as a journalist with a news-reporting agency at London's Heathrow Airport. The comings and goings of politicians and personalities were part of our daily bread and butter, along with industrial disputes and 'human interest' stories.

One day around 1970, a photographer and I were walking through the airport's European Terminal as part of our daily round, visiting contacts and keeping our eyes open for story opportunities. Fog had descended on Heathrow during the night and everything was at a standstill, stranding thousands of passengers in overcrowded departure lounges. One of them was Orson Welles.

We couldn't have missed him if we had tried. There he was, larger than life, wearing black from his fedora-clad head down past a dramatic cape to his boots – Charles Foster Kane, Sir John Falstaff, Harry Lime, the voiceover for Bird's Eye peas and fish fingers and the man who had scared America over three decades before.

Welles sat in the crowded lounge, wedged between multitudes of other stranded passengers, puffing on a large cigar (those were the days when you could smoke just about anywhere inside an airport). He looked distracted and disgruntled, probably wondering why he had not been invited into an airline VIP lounge, away from the other travellers.

The photographer and I paused for a moment to take in the sight and decide how to approach the great man. Just then he looked in our direction, saw the camera, took a long puff on his cigar and for a few seconds vanished in a cloud of blue smoke. He knew that press people always hung out at airports; after all, several years before he had appeared in a film called *The VIPs*, which, coincidentally, had been set in Heathrow Airport closed by fog. He played the role of film producer pursued by a reporter (a young David Frost). Perhaps I would have more luck.

I was twenty-one in 1970 and loved the theatre and the cinema. I had seen Welles in *The Third Man* and many of his poorer films; movies he had appeared in to earn a living and fund projects he had written and wanted to direct. I had admired his performances in John Huston's *Moby Dick* and his own *Chimes at Midnight,* which, in my view, is his best work alongside *Citizen Kane.* Welles himself might not have been so proud of the other films I had seen him appear in at the local Majestic picture house – *Ferry to Hong Kong, The Tartars* and *The Roots of Heaven.* But I knew and admired his work and would tell him so if he granted me an interview.

We approached him with a cheery, 'Good morning Mr Welles, nice weather we're having today.' He gave a grunt and I introduced myself. The elderly lady sitting next to him stood up and left and I quickly slipped into her seat and produced my notebook.

'I've got nothing to say, I've got no news,' said Welles. 'I'm waiting to get on a plane to Paris but because of this dammed fog, I'm stuck here.' He refused to answer any of my other questions about why he was travelling to Paris, what he'd been doing in London, and what his future plans were. I even asked about his 1938 radio dramatisation of *The War of the Worlds,* which had just been released on a pair of LP vinyl records for the first time since its original broadcast. But Welles was having none of it. 'Look, I don't want to say anything, so if you wouldn't mind, I'd rather be left alone.'

My photographer had already fired off a few photographs of Welles and flashes from his camera had been noticed by other passengers, who came over to gawp at what was going on. Those sitting near Welles knew exactly who he was, but none had approached him to ask for autographs or be photographed with him. Perhaps his dark, brooding exterior had put them off.

So I thanked him and put out my hand. He gently shook it. My photographer had his picture, but I had no story. Shortly afterwards we came across the Air France VIP lounge manager and asked him why Welles had not been invited inside. 'He's travelling economy. We only allow first class passengers into the lounge.' I said that it might be good public relations for the airline if they made an exception in his case and pointed to where Welles was sitting, still puffing on his cigar.

The VIP manager went across and Welles rose from his seat like a gigantic helium-filled balloon and followed him to the lounge. As he passed us he smiled and I think he knew we were responsible for rescuing him from economy class hell.

My second Welles encounter took place at Heathrow eighteen months later. A group of us were crossing the road from one terminal to another when we spied Welles standing on the kerbside next to a mountain of luggage, obviously waiting for someone to collect him. Again he saw us (it is difficult to miss a gaggle of pressmen, many with cameras slung over their shoulders) and fired an angry look in our direction. But we kept on walking, as we were on our way to another story. He was probably pleased, but I was disappointed at not getting an interview for the second time.

My third and final encounter was thirteen years later, in 1984, and this time in St Louis, where I was changing planes from London en route to Los

Angeles. While sitting with other passengers waiting to be called to the plane, a pair of double side doors opened and a member of the airline's staff entered, pushing a very large man in a wheelchair. It was Orson Welles, as usual dressed in black. There must have been around a hundred passengers waiting to board the plane and half of them noticed who he was immediately.

The wheelchair was pushed towards an empty space near where first class passengers would shortly be boarding the plane. Several people came up to him and one said she had enjoyed seeing him on television the previous evening. 'You really made my night,' said another, 'thank you for your wonderful work, Mr Welles.' He politely thanked them before being allowed to board the aircraft in his wheelchair before the other passengers.

He didn't notice me. Why should he? It's not as if we were friends. He didn't know me, but I felt I knew him thanks to his great body of work and some superb performances (and a few duff ones, too) in a handful of great films – one of them perhaps the greatest American film ever made.

This book is the story of one small part of the early life of George Orson Welles (1915–85), who – as Marlene Dietrich says of Welles' character, Hank Quinlan, at the close of his underrated film classic *Touch of Evil* – 'was some kind of man'.

ORSON WELLES AND MERCURY THEATRE ON THE AIR

SUNDAY OCTOBER 30, 1938
8:00 to 9:00 P.M.

CUE:                    (COLUMBIA BROADCASTING SYSTEM)
                       (.........30 seconds.........)

ANNC'R:        The Columbia Broadcasting System and its affiliated

               stations present Orson Welles and the Mercury

               Theatre on the Air in "The War of the Worlds" by

               H. G. Wells.

THEME:                                                            *30*

ANNC'R:        Ladies and Gentlemen, the director of the Mercury

               Theatre and star of these broadcasts, Orson Welles....


                       (WELLES SPEAKS)



*Note - Th*              This script of my radio play
                        WAR OF THE WORLDS was one
                        used in the broadcast....
                        Corections made by Orson
                        Welles.

                        ___ Howard Koch.

The title page of Howard Koch's typewritten script of *The War of the Worlds*, auctioned at Sotheby's in 1988. Handwritten amendments by Orson Welles and the CBS censor (see appendix on page 152).

# CHAPTER ONE

# When Radio Was King

*'Today there are millions of people who don't even know what happened that Halloween night on the radio. Back then, radio was really big. It was also a big piece of furniture in our living rooms ... and it occupied a big piece of our lives.'*
—*Orson Welles, 1970*

It was the evening of Sunday 30 October 1938, the night before Halloween. For many, church had been dutifully attended, grass cut for the last time that year and autumn leaves raked from the lawn. The car had been cleaned on the driveway, sports pages devoured for latest news about the Yankees, a good roast chicken dinner eaten, coffee swallowed, and dishes washed and returned to their cupboards.

Many parents had ventured out into the early evening hours with young ones dressed as witches, wizards, skeletons and ghosts. While they stood back, children nervously knocked on doors opened by friends and neighbours who pretended to shriek in horror when they saw what was standing on their doorstep asking 'Trick or treat?' The Halloween brigade was rewarded with candy or a cookie before they headed home again. And as they approached their houses or apartments, they saw pumpkins, hollowed out and carved and with a traditional face illuminated by a small candle, positioned inside their windows.

Now it was time to settle down to America's favourite pastime. The radio was switched on for a relaxing evening of popular music, comedy and drama enjoyed by the entire family; it was a chance to escape for a while from news about political unrest in Europe and the economic depression that had swept across the country, turning the American Dream into a nightmare for tens of thousands of citizens.

By 1938, radio had reached the zenith of its popularity. The medium was so popular and powerful that American novelist and social commentator Sinclair Lewis called radio 'the third ear of the human race'. Despite the economic slump, there were 27.5 million 'radio homes' in America with eight out of

By 1938, radio had peaked in popularity in the United States. 80 per cent of Americans tuned in daily. (*The Library of Congress*)

ten people tuning in daily. At that time the United States' population of 138 million needed something to help them forget that 25 per cent of its adult workforce was unemployed. But instead of listening to songs on the air, like 'Brother Can You Spare a Dime?' and its famous lines

> Once I built a railroad, made it run,
> Made it race against time.
> Once I built a railroad – now it's done.
> Brother, can you spare a dime…?

they were hearing another song that suggested better times might be just around the corner:

> Happy days are here again,
> The skies above are clear again,
> Let us sing a song of cheer again –
> Happy days are here again…

A song by George and Ira Gershwin made popular by Fred Astaire the previous year had the ironic title 'Nice Work if You Can Get It'. The song was written as a boy-loves-girl piece, but its plaintive chorus could have been written about life for many Americans in the closing years of the third decade of the twentieth century:

Nice work if you can get it,
And you can get it if you try.

And later:

Nice work if you can get it,
And if you get it –
Won't you tell me how?

This was something millions wanted to know – how and where to find jobs when there were none. Fear stalked the United States in the autumn of 1938. Although President Roosevelt had told Americans that they 'had nothing to fear but fear itself', there were few signs that the Great Depression might be coming to an end and confidence returning. 8 million Americans remained unemployed and others feared that war-like threats coming from the other side of the Atlantic might plunge the country into deeper economic gloom, making it difficult to pay mortgages, rent or domestic bills, or even buy groceries from the general store.

The news from Europe was far from good. Germany had already marched into neighbouring Austria; the swastika was flying over public buildings in Vienna and Austrian Jews were given notice by their employers. On 29 September the leaders of Britain, France, Italy and Germany met in Munich to discuss Hitler's claim to Czechoslovakia's Sudeten territories and to hold back the looming spectre of war. Britain's Neville Chamberlain flew home, waved a piece of paper in the air and promised, 'Peace in our time.' Five days later Hitler's troops marched into the Sudetenland.

Although unrest promised to wreck the Thanksgiving Day plans of millions, a quick tour of the Sunday 30 October 1938 edition of *The New York Times* – twelve sections, 100 pages and all for 10¢ – shows that while confidence and prosperity had not returned to the entire country, it was abundant in the nation's most prosperous metropolis. Advertising space in the paper far outweighs those columns given over to news. The first section is dominated by page after page of promotional space for women's fashion, cosmetics and home décor.

Hearn's department store reminded readers that 'America is on the way up – and with the country at last definitely on the "up-grade" with boom conditions steadily materialising, Hearn's is on the march, too, with $6 million worth of exciting new bargains for everybody! Hearn's is the bargain store for all the people! You'll remember November at Hearn's!'

Stern Brothers tempted female readers with a promise that 'this fur coat is worth $1,000 – but tomorrow we'll sell it for $495!' Mis-Chief by Vogue promised the same audience 'a new kind of All-in-One that up's your bosom and pulls your tummy flat – a bargain at just $10'.

Other big stores organised pre-Thanksgiving Day sales. McCreery's offered $124,000 worth of oriental rugs for $59,000 – 'a sale of dramatic scope' – and Saks at 34th Street promised Coty's Eau de Toilette in the eight-ounce economy size for just $2.95. Macy's – 'helping you to live better for less' – slashed 63 per cent off a range of stainless steel pots and pans and brought the cost of simulated leather chairs down to the 'sensational price' of $7.98 each.

In between advertisements, the news section was predictably bleak. The paper reported that while Germany had ceased the mass deportation of Polish Jews pending further negotiations between Warsaw and Berlin, Germany's foreign minister, Joachim von Ribbentrop, had met Italy's Premier Mussolini in Rome and signed an agreement 'on the Hungro-Czech problem.'

*The New York Times Magazine* reflected on the storm clouds gathering over Europe with a feature about 'the four big men who hold the fate of Europe in their hands'. The four were identified as Neville Chamberlain ('a perfect type of Victorian'), Adolf Hitler ('a dreamer and bitter fanatic'), Benito Mussolini ('as level headed as he is robust') and Eduard Daladier ('the French peasant with a quick mind'). Next to the article, and to remind Americans that what was happening on the other side of the Atlantic was really none of their concern, was an advertisement for the new Pontiac Silver Streak – '... the most beautiful thing on wheels. Easy payment terms available.'

At home, the biggest domestic story of the day told readers that there were 'just 74 more days until *Gone With the Wind* goes before the cameras – Tara has already been built, but the role of Miss Scarlett O'Hara is yet to be cast after a two-and-a-half year search. Just who the lady of destiny will be is still in the lap of the Gods.'

Going to see a Hollywood movie at least once every week was America's second favourite pastime after listening to the radio. By 1938, there were over 17,000 movie theatres in the United States drawing around 88 million people every week. Film fans went to the movies to swoon over Clark Gable, Bette Davis, Greta Garbo, Errol Flynn, Fred Astaire and Ginger Rogers, Mickey Mouse, W. C. Fields, Bob Hope, the Marx Brothers and a curly-headed and dimpled moppet called Shirley Temple, who tap-danced and sang about 'the Good Ship Lollipop'.

But only radio allowed Americans to laugh in the comfort of their own houses, apartments, farms and shacks at the antics of Jack Benny, George Burns and Gracie Allen, Amos 'n' Andy, and Fibber McGee and Molly. In 1938, more American families had radios in their homes than had telephones, cars, plumbing, electricity or subscriptions to newspapers or magazines. Radio was king.

Mini-dramas – called 'soap operas' because detergent manufacturers commercially sponsored them – dominated daytime airwaves. A show called *Our Gal Sunday* began each episode with the question, 'Can a girl from a little mining town in the west find happiness as the wife of a wealthy and titled

Englishman?' Many a girl's ear was glued to her radio every day hoping to learn the answer. The heroics of the Lone Ranger, the Green Hornet, the Shadow and 'All-American Boy' Jack Armstrong thrilled listeners of all ages – and, thanks to a breakfast cereal sponsor, helped sell millions of boxes of Corn Flakes.

President Franklin Roosevelt recognised the power of radio during the early days of his administration and used the medium regularly for his famous 'fireside chats'. Roosevelt began his broadcasts with the phrase 'Good evening, friends,' and went on to speak about the burning issues of the day, including his New Deal programme, unemployment, drought, and the need for faith in the country's banking system. The chance for Americans to be addressed directly by the president himself, through their radios, helped Roosevelt influence American public opinion and accept his political reforms.

One of the most dramatic moments in the history of radio and the cinema newsreels occurred on 6 May 1937, when the German airship *Hindenburg* burst into flames as it was about to land in Lakehurst, New Jersey. WLS Chicago radio reporter Herb Morrison conveyed the horror of the incident. Millions shared his horrific reaction to what was happening in front of him through their radio sets. They later witnessed the *Hindenburg* horror for themselves when they went to the movies and heard his commentary all over again, dubbed onto a newsreel soundtrack.

President Franklin D. Roosevelt used radio to broadcast his regular 'Fireside Chats'. (© *Bettmann/CORBIS*)

Evening radio listening began early in 1938. For people living in the eastern states, from Maine down to Florida and Massachusetts across to Indiana, 7 p.m. was the time to switch on and settle down. Programmes went on until late, long after children had been tucked up in bed, while mom and pop enjoyed a little quiet time together for the first time that day.

But as American families from Maine to California settled around radio sets on the evening of Sunday 30 October 1938, they had no idea that for many thousands across their country, something so shocking, so heart-stopping, so horrific, so unbelievable, so inconceivable was about to happen right there in their own living rooms.

They forgot about the economy, war cries from Europe, Macy's sale and Scarlett O'Hara, because this was the night hostile aliens from a distant plant would invade Earth and attempt to conquer the United States of America – and its people…

# CHAPTER TWO

# Mr Welles Meets
# Mr Houseman

'*Well, peace be with you, sir: here comes my man.*'
—*Tybalt in Shakespeare's* Romeo and Juliet

In December 1934 a thirty-three-year-old aspiring theatrical producer called John Houseman slipped a 50¢ bit into the hand of a stage doorman at the rear of Broadway's Martin Beck Theatre and persuaded him to give directions as to where the young actor playing the role of Tybalt that night in Katherine Cornell's production of Shakespeare's *Romeo and Juliet* might be found.

Houseman deliberately arrived late, knowing that by 10 p.m. Tybalt would have been stabbed by Romeo (played by a middle-aged Basil Rathbone) in Verona's sunlit square and the actor appearing in the role, a nineteen-year-old unknown called Orson Welles, would be sitting in his dressing room waiting for his curtain call.

The *Romeo and Juliet* cast featured Miss Cornell herself as Juliet and British players Edith Evans and Brian Aherne as the Nurse and Mercutio. Houseman had attended the opening night several days earlier and was unimpressed by what he had seen on stage until the actor cast as Tybalt entered 'in a spring of such furious energy that, once released, it could be stopped by no human intervention'. For Houseman, Orson Welles' initial impact 'was overwhelming and unforgettable'. He recalled the actor's 'pale, shiny child's face under the unnatural growth of dark beard, from which there issued a voice of such clarity and power that it tore like a high wind through the genteel, modulated voices of the well-trained professionals around him'.

The stage doorman led the way up a dark flight of stairs and along a narrow corridor, from where Houseman could hear lines from the play's final act rising faintly from somewhere below. He was shown to a cramped and cluttered cubicle in which the wonder boy himself, 'naked to the waist sat before his mirror under the glaring bulbs, waiting for his long-delayed curtain call. His black-and-scarlet Tybalt costume, stiff and heavy with sweat, lay over the back of a chair.' The young actor had removed his crêpe-hair beard but had retained his false nose and was in the process of repairing his make-up before going down to take his bow.

The budding producer and young actor agreed to meet half an hour later in a bar across the street from the theatre. When the youthful Welles walked in, Houseman failed to recognise the actor without his Tybalt costume and make-up. At around 6 feet, Welles was taller than he remembered. He had combed his hair and wore a dark, sober suit. Over whiskey cocktails, Houseman had his first opportunity to study the young actor at close quarter. He noticed 'a pale pudding face with violent black eyes, the button nose and the well-shaped mouth over astonishingly small teeth'. In the dim light of the booth where they consumed their drinks, Houseman was again conscious of the actor's voice that made people at neighbouring tables turn – 'startled not so much by its loudness as by its surprising vibration'.

Houseman told Welles that he had bought the rights to a new verse play about the 1929 Wall Street Crash called *Panic* (a prophetic title, bearing in mind the national panic the pair would create a few years later). It was penned by the Pulitzer Prize-winning poet and modernist author Archibald MacLeish.

Houseman announced that he intended to stage *Panic* in New York with his newly created Phoenix Theatre Company. According to Houseman, the play was 'patently uncommercial and presented obvious and apparently insurmountable production problems'. Yet by his own admission, Houseman was a man who would undertake what no one else would venture – and *Panic* was the perfect vehicle for such a demonstration. All that was needed was a strong actor with a striking stage presence to play the leading role of a doomed tycoon called McGafferty, described by MacLeish as 'the owner of the country's principal industries and greatest bank; the leading industrialist and financier of his time'. He was also billed in the script as 'a man in his late fifties' – and here was Houseman discussing the role with an actor not yet twenty years old.

Houseman asked Welles to tell him something about his life before joining Katherine Cornell's troupe. George Orson Welles revealed that he hailed from Kenosha, Wisconsin, where he was born in 1915, the second son of inventor Richard Welles, who had invented, among other things, a mechanical dishwasher that smashed all the crockery to pieces and a collapsible picnic set, purchased by the government in great quantities for US infantrymen and which, according to son Orson, 'greatly contributed to the horrors of the war'. He became an alcoholic and died when Orson was fifteen. His mother, a major influence, was a skilled pianist who introduced him to Shakespeare, the piano and the violin. Mr and Mrs Welles divorced when Orson was six years old.

Welles junior claimed he had made his theatrical debut at the age of ten, when he appeared at a Chicago department store in the role of Peter Rabbit for $25 a day. At twelve he was enrolled in the progressive Todd School for Boys in Woodstock, Illinois, where he staged his first production of *Julius Caesar* and played the roles of the Soothsayer, Cassius and Mark Anthony.

After graduating from the Todd School in 1931 and with no family home to return to, the young student set out on a painting and walking tour of Ireland with $500 in his pocket. In Dublin, young Welles talked his way into the city's Gate Theatre, claiming he was a Broadway actor. The theatre's actor-manager, Hilton Edwards, failed to believe him but was impressed by his bravura style and gave the lad a role in a new production of *Jew Süss*. Welles turned in an impressive performance and word of mouth about the young 'Broadway star' travelled back across the Atlantic.

A chance introduction to writer Thornton Wilder at a cocktail party led Welles to the American stage in 1933 as a member of Katherine Cornell's company and appearances in touring productions of *Romeo and Juliet* (in which he played the Chorus and Mercutio), Shaw's *Candida* (playing Eugene Marchbanks) and *The Barretts of Wimpole Street* (in the role of Octavius Barrett). Critics hailed young Welles as 'the new wunderkind of American theatre'. But the wunderkind was outraged when a planned Broadway season of *Romeo and Juliet* was cancelled, forcing him to return to his old school, where he staged a theatre festival featuring Michael MacLiammoir and Hilton Edwards from the Gate Theatre, Dublin. It was a tremendous success and Cornell summoned 'wonderboy' back to New York to appear as Tybalt when her all-star *Romeo and Juliet* finally came to Broadway.

It was time for Houseman to tell the young maestro something of himself. He had been born Jacques Haussmann in Romania thirty-three years before, the son of a British mother and an Alsatian-born Jewish father who ran a grain business. His parents changed their family name to 'Houseman' before sending their son to England to study at Clifton College, Bristol, where he acquired the cultured English accent he retained for the rest of his life.

His first job was working for his father's business, which in 1925 took him to the United States. He decided to stay. In addition to selling grain, Houseman wrote short stories for magazines and translated articles from French and German. By the 1930s he had drifted into the theatrical world, acquiring a reputation as an 'all-rounder' – author, director, writer and producer.

By now Welles and Houseman knew enough about each other to be comfortable. Welles took the *Panic* script home along with Houseman's telephone number. He called the following day, said he wanted to play McGafferty and asked, 'When do rehearsals begin?'

The next day Houseman summoned Welles to meet MacLeish at the tiny single room office he rented above a burlesque theatre. When the nineteen-year old walked in, MacLeish's eyes narrowed with exasperation. There were only two chairs in the grimy room, so Houseman squatted on the floor with his back to the wall, while Welles and MacLeish used chairs.

On hearing Welles' deep *basso profondo* voice, MacLeish immediately changed his mind and by the end of the reading had agreed that this was the perfect – and only – actor for the demanding role of McGafferty. He also advanced Houseman the necessary capital needed to mount the play and stage it at Broadway's Imperial Theatre – better known for musical comedy than verse-drama – for three performances, plus seven days for rehearsal and set building.

*Panic* offered roles for twenty-five actors and twenty-three chorus speakers. Scenes were set in offices and city streets with electric news bulletin boards announcing each day's Wall Street dealings in moving lights. Houseman persuaded his friend Jo Mielziner, one of the New York theatre's leading stage designers, to work for free designing and building the set. To choreograph the cast, dance director Martha Graham was also persuaded to work for nothing, while composer Virgil Thomson agreed to write music for a knockdown fee of $50. A New York theatre columnist wrote that Houseman had succeeded in 'beguiling a large company of excellent and willing actors into donating their services to an unusual artistic cause'. In other words, they were appearing for next to nothing in order to be seen in a prestigious original production by one of the country's most fashionable poets.

Houseman estimated he would only recoup the $4,500 production costs providing each of the three scheduled performance was a sell-out. But despite mixed reviews, *Panic* lost its investors – and MacLeish – a sizeable sum of money. However, it opened unexpected new doors for its leading actor.

Houseman had arranged for excerpts from *Panic* to be broadcast on a radio arts programme and although it failed to ignite much interest at the Imperial Theatre box office, it introduced young Welles to a medium perfect for his talents – particularly his unique voice. Following the broadcast, Welles was hired by actor and director Paul Stewart to take part in *The American School of the Air*, a half-hour educational series broadcast by CBS on weekday afternoons. Programmes were transmitted across the country to 100,000 classrooms, in which sat 3 million children.

Thanks to *The American School of the Air*, Welles joined a large band of anonymous actors who earned a living rushing from one New York studio to another, appearing in different radio programmes. Radio actors were often asked to record as many as six programmes in a single day. Fortunately the recording studios of rival stations CBS and NBC were close to each other.

In a 1982 BBC interview, Welles remembered:

> I used to go by ambulance from one radio station to another, because I discovered there was no law in New York stating that you had to be sick to travel in an ambulance. So I hired the ambulance and I would go from CBS to NBC. They'd hold an elevator for me; I'd go up to the fifth floor, go into the studio, whichever I was booked for. I'd say, 'What's the character?' They'd say, 'Eighty-year-old Chinaman,' and I'd go on and do the eighty-year-old Chinaman, and then rush off somewhere else. And I had been for a year and a half auditioning hopelessly as an actor. Never could get a job on

'Radio is a popular, democratic machine for disseminating information and entertainment, but as regards drama it is still in the experimental stage,' Welles told *The New York Times* in August 1938. (*Author's Collection*)

radio. Suddenly, I got one part and in about a month I was making, in those days, tax-free, about $1,500 to $1,800 a week, as an unknown radio actor, without my name being mentioned.

As well as radio dramas, Welles also provided voiceovers for the weekly radio documentary feature *The March of Time*. The radio medium brought Welles into contact with players with whom he would soon be working in different circumstances – including Joseph Cotton, Ray Collins, George Coulouris, Erskine Sanford, Everett Slone and Agnes Moorhead.

Radio engagements also bought Welles time to plan his next move in November 1934 – his marriage to Virginia Nicholson, a red-headed socialite and actress he had met when they had appeared together at drama festivals the previous year. Radio earnings paid for a single-room basement apartment on New York's Riverside Drive, where they lived together in bohemian splendor.

The future looked good for the new Mr and Mrs Welles and their new friend Mr Houseman. Although they didn't know it at the time, exciting times lay ahead…

# CHAPTER THREE

# *Macbeth* and *The Cradle Will Rock*

*'... and when the wind blows, the cradle will rock!'*
*—Mark Blitzstein, 1937*

It was time for Welles and Houseman to begin planning their next move. They met regularly to discuss plays they might produce, theatres in which to stage them and actors to cast. Welles' newfound financial independence bought him time to consider his next artistic endeavour, but Houseman's need to generate cash to prop up his dwindling savings was more urgent.

Help arrived in the form of the Federal Theatre Project – known as the FTP – an ambitious effort mounted by Roosevelt's government to organise and produce theatrical events that would employ out-of-work theatre people, including actors, dancers, directors, playwrights, choreographers, designers, vaudeville artists, musicians and stage technicians, to create vital theatre for communities damaged by the depression.

Although administered from Washington, DC, FTP companies stretched the full breadth of the country. They operated on limited budgets, often playing in factories, barns and cinemas as well as theatres, many of which had been dark since the start of the depression. Actors and backstage crew each earned $20 per week. Many were said to be communists and many shows were politically left-wing, with strong bias towards the spirit of Roosevelt's New Deal. Between 1935 and 1939, the FTP employed over 12,000 men and women and played to over 30 million Americans paying just a few cents each to watch plays in over 200 different performing areas. Funding was eventually terminated, but in that brief period, the project was responsible for some of the most innovative staging of its time – and Welles and Houseman were responsible for presenting some of the most innovative shows.

Houseman's involvement came about after he was asked if he might be interested in helping found an FTP branch for New York-based black performers. He recalled later that the term 'black' was generally taboo and 'negro' was in official and general use. The theatre group would be based in

Harlem, a district Houseman had hardly visited. He recalled that a corrosive misery filled its streets and houses. Harlem had a church on every corner and the highest crime rate in New York.

While Houseman was putting the new company together – he was the only non-black person involved with the enterprise – Welles was busy appearing in a long-running radio series called *The Shadow*, playing the role of crime fighter Lamont Cranson, a wealthy playboy who used hypnotic powers to conquer evil under the pseudonym of 'the Shadow'.

The radio mysteries were among America's most popular shows. Although not the first actor to play Lamont Cranson, Welles became the best-known. Each show began with the Shadow himself confiding to his audience, 'Heh-heh-heh-heh-heh! Who knows what evil lurks in the hearts of men? The Shadow knows! Heh-heh-heh-heh-heh!'

An announcer then added, 'The Shadow, a mysterious character who aids the forces of law and order, is, in reality, Lamont Cranston, wealthy young man-about-town. Years ago in the Orient, Lamont learned the strange and hypnotic power that allowed him to cloud men's minds so that they cannot see him. Lamont's companion, the lovely Margo Lane, is the only one that knows to whom the voice of the invisible Shadow belongs.'

Each programme ended with Shadow warning any crooks that had tuned into the show, 'The weed of crime bears bitter fruit. Crime does not pay. The shadow knows. Heh-heh-heh-heh!'

*The Shadow* featured many players Welles had already appeared alongside on radio, including Agnes Moorhead (in the role of Margo Lane), Ray Collins (as Commissioner Weston), Paul Stewart and Everett Sloane – actors who would go on to become an integral part of Welles' later career in radio, theatre and cinema.

Houseman recalled that the suggestion of mounting an all-black production of Shakespeare's *Macbeth* set on the voodoo island of Haiti arrived in an early morning telephone call from Welles, who said that his wife, Virginia, had come up with the original idea. On the spot Houseman invited Welles to direct it. And so it was that the second non-black person to join the FTP's Negro Theatre was recruited.

Few black actors at that time had experience working with Elizabethan verse and word soon got onto the street that Houseman and Welles had dreamt up a white man's scheme in order to degrade black people. Nothing could have been further from the truth. Welles wanted to work with raw material and that is exactly what walked through the door when auditions were announced.

The final cast for the voodoo melodrama numbered 137, with central roles played by experienced performers who were nevertheless inexperienced in speaking the iambic pentameters penned by a white man who had lived thousands of miles away. Houseman described the cast as 'an amazing mishmash of amateurs and professionals, church members and radicals, sophisticates and wild ones, adherents of Father Devine and bushmen from darkest Africa'. The cast also included a troupe of African drummers and an authentic witch doctor.

The company arrived for rehearsals wanting to try something new; they were putty in Welles' chubby hands. They did everything he asked of them and offered their own suggestions about making the voodoo theme more authentic. Welles was delighted and incorporated many of these ideas into his direction, winning over the cast with the sheer force of his personality.

Houseman said that the FTP's voodoo *Macbeth* was probably the first full-scale, all-professional black Shakespearian production ever staged in American theatrical history. To bring it to life, Welles was forced to work a punishing schedule, interrupting rehearsals two and sometimes three times daily to jump into his ambulance from Harlem down to Manhattan to play the Shadow and take other radio jobs. As soon as he came off air, he jumped back into the ambulance to rush back uptown to rejoin his cast and wrestle with what was fast becoming a very original interpretation of *Macbeth*. At the end of the day he would return to Virginia to snatch a few hours sleep before dashing back to Harlem early the next day to work with the cast, composer, costume designer, lighting director and voodoo drummers.

The company members were all dirt poor and, knowing their director was earning a small fortune from radio engagements, were unafraid to tap him on the shoulder for loans or handouts. In addition to helping out his cast financially, Welles dug into his own pockets for additional props and costumes for the show.

Three days before opening night at Harlem's New Lafayette Theatre, the district awoke to find 'Macbeth' stenciled in luminous paint on every street corner from Lexington to Broadway. Tickets went on sale and every seat was sold within hours – prices ranging from 15¢ to 40¢. Even big Broadway theatre critics promised to attend, although one sent a note asking the FTP not to seat him and his wife 'next to any Negroes'.

The following day's notices were ecstatic and the show played to standing room only for its entire ten weeks at the New Lafayette before moving downtown to Broadway, where success continued. The production then went on tour, but in Indianapolis the actor playing Macbeth fell ill. Fortunately Welles had no radio commitments that week, and hastily jumped onto the first train to Indianapolis and played the role himself in blackface for the rest of the run.

\* \* \*

Houseman now began to ponder his own future. *Macbeth* had been such an adventure for all concerned, and he was unsure how to top its success. One thing was certain: he wanted to continue working with the boy genius who had moulded the show, in expectation that further theatrical triumphs awaited them. But Welles was impatient and Houseman knew that he was already dreaming of new worlds to conquer and had no intention of undertaking another long grind in Harlem that, at best, could only bring a repetition of their first triumph.

Two paths lay before Houseman. The first was to allow Welles to go off on his dazzling way while he remained at the head of the FTP's Negro Theatre; the second was to resign while the company was at the peak of its success, turn it over to 'those to whom it rightly belonged', and risk his future on a partnership with the energetic actor 'in whose talent I had unquestioning faith but with whom I must increasingly play the combined and tricky roles of producer, censor, advisor, impresario, father, older brother and bosom friend'.

He chose the latter after persuading the FTP to allow Welles and himself to create a new theatrical troupe based in the fading grandeur of Maxine Elliott's Theatre at 39th Street and Broadway, which the organisation was renting. As this would be the FTP's 891st theatrical venture, the company would be christened Project 891.

Houseman set up an office in the theatre's pink-painted basement powder room next to the ladies' toilets, while Welles moved into the star dressing room, complete with a bath, a small sitting room and a bed.

Hundreds of unemployed actors and backstage stage technicians applied to join Project 891's inaugural productions, which included new versions of Eugene Labiche's ninety-year-old French farce *The Italian Straw Hat* – renamed *Horse Eats Hat* – and a revival of Marlowe's 300-year-old tragedy *Doctor Faustus*, both to be directed by Welles. The former, starring young Joseph Cotton in the leading role, received mix reviews from the critics but the public at large, paying 55¢ for tickets, lapped it up. The latter starred Welles in the central role of the man who sells his soul to the devil for power, knowledge and material gain. The show was another enormous popular hit and played to over 80,000 people during its four-month Broadway run.

Next in line was the world premiere of Marc Blitzstein's curious, political 'play with music' *The Cradle Will Rock*. The piece, sung-through, had been written in just five weeks following the advent of Roosevelt's New Deal. Welles had fallen in love with Blitzstein's music and script and the author was totally bowled over by Welles' brilliance and power.

The piece perfectly captured the mood of 1937. Although Americans were unaware of the fact, this was a time of transition between the end of the Great Depression and the beginning of a gathering industrial boom that was to accompany the country's preparations for the Second World War. It was also the year that labour unrest vied for space with international news in American newspapers. Strikes had closed automobile factories in the Midwest, steel mills were picketed, and workers fought the police, who used guns, clubs and tear gas to repel strikers. Policemen shot ten strikers, seven of them in the back.

From the start of rehearsals, *The Cradle Will Rock* began sending out signals that this was no ordinary piece of Broadway musical theatre. Inspired by the approach, words and music of the German partnership of Bertolt Brecht and Kurt Weill, now both living in exile in the United States, the piece was designed as an allegory of corruption and corporate greed in 1930s America.

Set in the fictional industrial community of 'Steeltown, USA', Blitzstein's creation focused on the efforts of his central character, Larry Foreman, to unionise a company run by corrupt businessman 'Mr Mister'. The show featured a raft of characters including Mr Mister's outwardly genteel (yet inwardly vicious) philanthropist wife, his children, artists, near-bankrupt shopkeepers, immigrants, a faithless priest and a local prostitute called Moll.

For the leading roles, Welles and Houseman hired a pair of actors known for their outspoken political views. Will Geer (who would become known much later as Grandpa Walton in the TV series *The Waltons*) was engaged for the role of Mr Mister, while Howard da Silva, a former steelworker, would play Larry Foreman. Thirteen years later both actors would be blacklisted for refusing to testify before the House Committee on Un-American Activities and reveal names of fellow actors and directors known to be communist sympathisers. The parts they were to play to critical acclaim in *The Cradle Will Rock* would hardly go in their favour in later years.

Houseman recalled that the style of the piece as it took shape in rehearsals fell somewhere between realism, vaudeville and oratory, with the singing ranging from arias to patter and the blues. He remembered:

> Almost from the first day [of rehearsals] there were strange, prophetic stirrings in the air – a turbulence that grew with the weeks as the harsh realities of the national crisis met the rising theatrical excitement that was being generated on our bare, worklit stage. As opening night approached, those winds reached tornado force. How they finally flew *The Cradle Will Rock* right out of our theatre onto another stage twenty blocks uptown has become part of American theatrical history.

Rumours that FTP budgets were to be cut began circulating. There were whispers that the overtly left-wing political tones contained in many productions and the political leanings of many actors, directors and composers had made the organisation an enemy of right-wing congressmen. While no direct mention was made of the productions staged by Project 891, other FTP shows had lampooned living politicians and foreign heads of state – familiar today, but less common in the American theatrical world of the 1930s.

As the first night of *The Cradle Will Rock* approached, many FTP players went on a twenty-four-hour strike to protest the threatened cuts. Days later, 1,700 FTP actors, directors and technical staff were laid off and the organisation's budget was cut by 30 per cent.

Project 891's *Cradle* cast of sixty players and twenty-eight musicians working on an elaborate set with a complicated lighting plot was scheduled to open at the Maxine Elliot on 16 June 1937. With ten days to go before curtain up and 10,000 advance tickets sold, a memo landed on Houseman's desk informing him – and other FTP directors – that 'because of impending cuts and reorganisation, any new play, musical performance or art gallery' was forbidden to open before July.

Welles took a fast train to Washington to plead Project 891's case and threatened that if *Cradle* failed to open under government auspices, he and Houseman would launch it privately. Back in New York, the dress rehearsal went ahead, as planned. After the curtain fell, the lights were turned out and theatre doors locked – for good.

When the company arrived for their opening night the following evening, they discovered it padlocked with uniformed guards surrounding the playhouse, refusing entry to everyone. They claimed to have orders to make sure no government-owned property was used or removed, including scenery, costumes and props. No actors were allowed on stage or into dressing rooms to collect personal items. They even impounded a toupee owned by Howard da Silva.

Houseman and Welles persuaded the guards to allow the company to gather in the basement office while it was decided what to tell the audience – and the theatre reviewers – who would soon be gathering on the pavement expecting to be admitted. Frantic telephone calls were made to other theatrical managements in the hope that an empty theatre could be found to take a scaled-down version of the show. Meanwhile messages were received from both the actors' and musicians' unions, informing the performers that if they wished to appear under Houseman and Welles' management, they needed new contracts, guarantees of employment, and payment in full for three weeks worth of rehearsals – otherwise they were forbidden to appear on any non-FTP stage.

'We felt betrayed and defeated,' Houseman remembered. 'We could give a show without scenery and costumes and, if need be, without an orchestra – but not without actors.'

An actor was sent out with $10 and told to buy a piano – any old piano. Later the actor reported back that a battered old upright had been found. He wanted to know where it was to be delivered. The actor was told to hire a truck and await further instructions.

By now word had spread that a bunch of actors had been locked out of their theatre on opening night and reporters and photographers arrived wanting the full story. It was time to face the press. Houseman takes up the story:

> Orson was radiating confidence. We told them that *The Cradle Will Rock* would be presented that night, as announced, even if Marc Blitzstein had to

perform it alone on a piano and sing all the parts. When they inquired where this tour de force would take place, we suggested they stay around and find out.

They were assured it would take place 'somewhere, somehow'.

Houseman and Welles told the company that their union had forbidden them to appear on stage but 'there is nothing to prevent you from entering whatever theatre we find, then getting up from your seats, as US citizens, and speaking or singing your piece when your cue comes'.

It was now 7.20 p.m. and the audience outside the theatre was becoming restless. Some actors went outside and performed impromptu scenes from the show in order to keep the punters calm.

Back inside, a small man in a dark hat who had been trying to attract the attention of Houseman and Welles for the last three hours said he couldn't understand what was wrong with the Venice Theatre – it was open, empty, available, cheap, and in every way suitable for their requirements. He turned out to be a theatre renting agent and he was holding a rusty key in his hand, which he said would admit them to the Venice Theatre on 7th Avenue at 58th Street at the cost of $100 for the night.

Within minutes, the piano was on its way to the theatre and Welles, Houseman and Blitzstein were marching actors and audience twenty-one city blocks to the new venue, inviting anyone they met on the way to way to join them as the Venice was three times larger than the padlocked playhouse.

Houseman recalled that there were no ticket takers that night, no ushers and no programmes. There would be no scenery, props or costumes and the lighting would be limited to a single spot. Curtain-up time had been changed to 9 p.m. but by 8.50 p.m. there was not an empty seat in the house. At 9.01 p.m. Welles and Houseman appeared in front of the Venice Theatre's shabby curtain. They thanked the audience for agreeing to take a long walk to the new theatre and explained the history of *The Cradle Will Rock* and what had happened to their company earlier that day. 'We told them we were not subversives, but artists fulfilling a commitment,' said Houseman. 'We told them how the show would have looked, sounded and described the characters they would not be seeing.'

In conclusion they announced, 'We now have the honour to present – with the composer at the piano – *The Cradle Will Rock*.'

The curtain rose to reveal Blitzstein alone on stage in his shirtsleeves sitting in the spotlight at the battered $10 upright piano. He began singing the opening number and one by one the actors joined in from their seats in the auditorium. And then as the story began to unfold, actors stood up in the stalls, the circle, the gallery, the boxes and down the aisles to say or sing their lines. Scenes and numbers followed each other in fantastic sequence with voices coming in from all parts of the theatre and the cast speaking and singing across the auditorium to each other. Audience members turned in their seats from one side of the theatre to another as if at a tennis tournament, and were thrilled by the experience.

The closing piece at the end of the show told the audience:

> When you can't climb down, and you can't sit still;
> That's a storm that's going to last until
> The final wind blows... And when the wind blows...
> The Cradle Will Rock!

When the actors spoke the final line in unison, all hell broke loose and the audience went wild. Cheering and applause lasted so long that stagehands demanded one hour's overtime – which they were paid. The next morning, *The Cradle Will Rock* was front-page news in every New York newspaper and ran for eleven packed performances at the Venice Theatre before returning to the Maxine Elliott Theatre after the FPA had been embarrassed enough to take their company back home.

It was shortly after this episode that Welles said to Houseman, 'Why the hell don't we start a theatre of our own?'

And Houseman replied, 'Why don't we?'

So they did. And they called it the Mercury Theatre Company.

# CHAPTER FOUR

# Mercury Rising

*'With a voice that booms like Big Ben but a laugh like a youngster's giggle, Orson Welles plays lead off stage as well as on.'*
—Time *magazine on Orson Welles, 1938*

The voodoo *Macbeth*, unconventional productions of *An Italian Straw Hat* and *Doctor Faustus*, and the revolutionary premiere of *The Cradle Will Rock* marked both Welles and Houseman out as theatrical mavericks guaranteed to take risks and create productions that would grab headlines, fill theatres and thrill audiences. Simon Callow, in his excellent biography of Orson Welles *The Road to Xanadu*, writes that at this time in his life, Welles 'was more than ever linked with notoriety, never a bad thing, as far as Welles was concerned'.

Welles and Houseman named the Mercury Theatre after reading an article in an old copy of the radical magazine *American Mercury*. The very name said it all – a bright planet, a shiny element that rises when subjected to pressure, a winged messenger… All things that the new theatrical venture aspired to become.

The Mercury Theatre, Inc., started life in the summer of 1937 with an ambitious programme of plays, a company of thirty-four actors and stage staff – each of whom would be paid $40 per week – and a budget of $9,000. Its home was a small, rotting, two-balcony rococo theatre with 687 seats and a decently sized stage on 41st Street and Broadway. Although known for some years at the Comedy and famous for small musicals, by the summer of 1937 it had stood empty for some time, was covered in cobwebs, and was, according to Houseman, 'home to rats the size of small dogs'.

The opening programme commenced with 'a modern production by Orson Welles' of Shakespeare's *Julius Caesar* – shortened to just *Caesar* – with Welles in the role of Brutus. Next would come Thomas Dekker's *The Shoemaker's Holiday* (again adapted by Welles) and Shaw's *Heartbreak House*. Actors invited to join the company included Joseph Cotton, George Coulouris, Norman Lloyd, Martin Gabel, Alice Frost, Virginia Welles (Mrs Orson Welles), Agnes Moorehead, Everett Sloane and Vincent Price.

Welles, still only twenty-two years old, now divided his time between directing the modern-dress *Caesar*, learning and rehearsing the part of Brutus, writing, directing and starring in a seven-part radio dramatisation of Victor Hugo's *Les Miserables* (in the role of the unfortunate Jean Valjean) and a new series of *The Shadow*. By now his name was well-known to New York theatre audiences. The identities of actors taking part in radio shows were rarely announced, although their voices were frequently recognised by listeners and playgoers. Welles, however, was an exception. By 1937 he was a member of an elite band of radio performers thanks to his rich voice and ability to convey an unlimited range of moods and emotions. As radio's highest-paid actor, his involvement in a production was often a means of attracting an audience. Frequently he was the only artist announced at the start or end of a programme, as its star, author or director – and sometimes all three. The remainder of the cast went without credit or acknowledgement, unless they were Broadway or Hollywood stars 'guesting' on a radio show.

Audiences and critics loved the Mercury's new version of *Caesar*, which dressed the cast in uniforms reminiscent of fascist Italy, drawing parallels between Julius Caesar and Benito Mussolini. Welles whittled Shakespeare's text down to ninety minutes, discarded several characters and ran the play through without an interval. Dialogue was moved around, lines were borrowed from other Shakespeare plays, and the last two acts were reduced to a single scene.

The production probably owed more to Welles than it did to Shakespeare, but *Variety* gave its review the headline 'Bard Boffola!' while *Time* magazine said the play had 'gone over with the loudest bang that Shakespeare-lovers could recall. And decidedly First in Rome had been Director Orson Welles for managing the entire production and Actor Orson Welles for making Brutus come alive in a blue-serge suit.'

At 157 performances, the Mercury production remains the longest-running version of *Julius Caesar* to play on Broadway. It later transferred to the Neiderlander Theatre on West 41st Street before touring the United States in 1938.

Three days after Welles celebrated his twenty-third birthday and six months after the Mercury's Broadway debut, both made their way into the pages of America's most successful and prestigious news magazine, *Time*. The publication's 9 May 1938 edition featured Welles on the front cover, in colour and in character as eighty-eight-year-old Captain Shotover in the Mercury's production of Shaw's *Heartbreak House*. Beneath the portrait was the caption, 'George Orson Welles – Shadow to Shakespeare, Shoemaker to Shaw'. Inside, a five-page profile of the young star under the headline 'Marvelous Boy' reflected on the Mercury's smash hits with *Caesar, The Cradle Will Rock* and 'a capital production' of *Heartbreak House*.

The *Time* feature was a publicity coup for the Mercury venture, described by the magazine as 'just an idea, bounded north & south by hope, east & west by nerve'. It was also an ego boost for Welles and nationwide recognition of his talent. *Time* cover stories usually featured the world's great politicians, heads of state, artists, authors and thinkers. Placing a young actor little known outside New York on its front page was a departure from tradition.

Telling its readers about Welles' early life, *Time* stated, 'Were Welles' 23 years set forth in fiction form, any self-respecting critic would damn the story as too implausible for serious consideration.' It added:

> With a voice that booms like Big Ben's but a laugh like a youngster's giggle, Orson Welles plays lead off stage as well as on. He loves the mounting Welles legend, but wants to keep the record straight. Stories of his recent affluence – the Big House at Sneden's Landing, NY, the luxurious Lincoln town car and chauffeur – annoy him. First of all, Welles insists, this has nothing to do with his Mercury triumphs; for years he has had these things by virtue of his radio earnings; and second, the Big House isn't such a big house (eight rooms and four nooks, $115 a month), the car is second-hand, and the chauffeur exists because Welles himself doesn't drive. Says he: 'I'm one of those fellows so frightened of driving that I go 80 miles an hour – and the more frightened I get, the faster I go.'

*Time* also said that Welles was 'as active as a malted-milk mixer'. He was here, there and everywhere, directing, adapting, acting, designing costumes, scenery and complicated lighting plots, writing programme notes, designing their covers, and giving interviews to New York newspapers.

\* \* \*

The Mercury Theatre was on its way. But at the end of its first season and after staging four successful shows in a row, it was nearly broke. While it had played to over a quarter of a million theatregoers, each paying less than $1 each for their seats, the cost of running a large company was challenging. On top of that, the Mercury had to pay rent for its theatre, had spent a small fortune decorating the building and clearing it of its rat population. While Houseman drew a small salary, Welles took no money from the Mercury's depleted coffers. He relied on radio fees to get by.

The Mercury closed its doors for the summer, giving Houseman and Welles time to begin planning their next season. Lack of funds meant that all new productions would have to be works penned by long-dead authors who demanded no royalties. There was also the need to reduce the number of actors in the company, downsize the season, and increase ticket prices to generate more cash at the box office.

And then in June 1938 a lifesaver came along in the form of the Columbia Broadcasting System – better known as CBS – who contacted Welles to ask if he might be interested in presenting the Mercury company in a different dramatic radio show every week for nine weeks, during which he could present anything he pleased.

The CBS boss was the legendary business tycoon William S. Paley, about whom *The New York Times* would later write, 'He is to American broadcasting as Carnegie was to steel, Ford to automobiles, Luce to publishing and Ruth to baseball.'

Paley had worked at his father's wholesale store, the La Palina Cigar Company, before entering broadcasting at the age of twenty-six after Paley Senior, a Ukrainian Jewish immigrant, had rescued a struggling Philadelphia network of sixteen radio stations called the Columbia Phonographic Broadcasting System with a $50,000 cash injection. The plan was to use the radio stations to promote the family cigar business, but Paley Jr had other ideas and the radio network soon grew into a profitable business thanks to advertising and sponsorship, allowing it to expand into 114 stations within a decade.

Although Welles' style of drama was not to Paley's personal taste, anyone who had appeared on the cover of *Time* magazine and featured so prominently in leading New York newspapers was definitely worth inviting in for a talk.

Welles took Houseman with him to meet CBS executives at the company's Manhattan studios at 485 Madison Avenue, a twenty-five-storey office

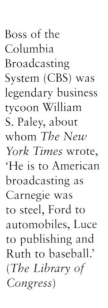

Boss of the Columbia Broadcasting System (CBS) was legendary business tycoon William S. Paley, about whom *The New York Times* wrote, 'He is to American broadcasting as Carnegie was to steel, Ford to automobiles, Luce to publishing and Ruth to baseball.' (*The Library of Congress*)

**WABC,** today, is New York's most familiar commodity: *more thoroughly distributed among New York homes than any other product you can name!*

*We've prepared a special study of New York radio stations and audiences for readers of this issue. Write to CBS, 485 Madison Ave., N. Y.*

**WABC** 50,000 WATTS · 860 KILOCYCLES

Owned and operated by the Columbia Broadcasting System, WABC is the key station of the world's largest radio network

*The Mercury Theatre of the Air*'s weekly drama series was aired by the CBS network's key flagship station WABC and transmitted to 150 other stations across America. (*Author's collection*)

building on the corner of Madison and 52nd Street. It was here that Paley had leased several floors, including studios, offices and technical facilities. Houseman, a man of the theatre, was keenly aware that he knew nothing about radio. Introduced by Welles as 'my associate at the Mercury Theatre', Houseman attempted to look knowledgeable about what was being discussed, but in truth, he was out of his depth.

Paley's executives spoke about their plan to present a drama season that would be aired by their key flagship station WABC to 150 other stations from coast to coast for one hour on Monday evenings at 8 p.m. Welles would have a free hand in selecting material, but the radio men urged him to consider presenting thrilling adventure stories suitable for family audiences – in other words, radio versions of classic stories but presented on air with a dash of Hollywood action. They heard that the series was being conceived as 'a prestige show of general appeal', in which Welles would introduce, narrate and close each programme as himself while also playing a leading character. The series was given the title *First Person Singular* and was scheduled to commence transmission on 11 July 1938 – less than a month away.

It would be up to Welles to select stories to be dramatised, commission writers, cast the shows, rehearse them and present them 'live' from Studio One on the twenty-second floor of the CBS Building. The show would use actors drawn from the Mercury's acting ranks, thus raising the theatre's profile across the entire United States, bringing its work into the home of every American owning a radio and seeking some form of dramatic entertainment every Monday evening.

The weekly dramas were to be mounted on a tight budget – $50,000 for nine shows or $5,500 per drama – from which Welles had to pay himself, his writers, actors and sound effects team. If he needed an orchestra, CBS would provide musicians from its own in-house resources. Unlike other popular shows on the CBS and NBC networks, the new series had yet to find a commercial sponsor to pay for its airtime. Houseman and Welles were told that this might change if their shows caught the attention of audiences large enough to attract a commercial sponsor with a fat chequebook – and CBS made it clear that a sponsor was expected to come forward if the show was to go to a second series.

With these words ringing in their ears, Welles and Houseman rode down the elevator and out into the roar of New York's traffic knowing that the opportunity placed on the table upstairs would give the Mercury Theatre, its actors and its star huge kudos with the American public – and a golden opportunity to fund their next theatrical repertory season.

While Welles and Houseman set about the dual task of organising the radio series and the next theatrical season, the name *First Person Singular* was quietly dropped in favour of another: *The Mercury Theatre on the Air*. The producer-partners thought it a much better title.

CHAPTER FIVE

# The Mercury Theatre
# on the Air

*'Radio is a popular, democratic machine for disseminating information and entertainment, but as regards drama it is still in the experimental stage.'*
—*Orson Welles in an interview with* The New York Times, *August 1938*

The Mercury's second season at its New York playhouse was as ambitious as its first: William Gillette's *Too Much Johnson* (with improvements by Welles), Georg Buchner's *Danton's Death* (adapted by Welles) plus an attempt (by Welles) to compress the best of Shakespeare's three 'Falstaff' plays into a single piece to be called *Three Kings* – with Welles himself in the leading role of colourful Sir John Falstaff. The season was designed to take the company up to the spring of 1939.

When not learning lines or rehearsing plays, Mercury cast members offered themselves up for any kind of role on the weekly radio dramas for a flat fee of $20 each. The first production was to be a swashbuckling adaptation of Robert Louis Stevenson's *Treasure Island* (with Welles playing a grown-up Jim Hawkins narrating the piece, plus the more showy part of peg-leg pirate Long John Silver).

Houseman, in his role as programme editor, spent a week attempting to adapt the novel into an hour-long radio play. He found the work hard going, having never created a radio drama before. Occasionally Welles would drop by to see how work was progressing, in between performing and clandestine visits to his latest mistress, the German-born ballerina Vera Zorina. And then, less than one week before the show was to be played across the American airwaves, Welles announced that instead of *Treasure Island*, *The Mercury Theatre on the Air* would debut with a new version of Bram Stoker's Gothic horror novel *Dracula*. Houseman takes up the story:

While I sent out for six copies of the book, Orson stayed long enough to describe his favourite scenes and departed. The next afternoon, two days before the start of rehearsals, he returned and we started to go over what I

Before the first play produced by *The Mercury Theatre on the Air* was broadcast, an announcer informed listeners that Orson Welles 'has come to be the most famous name in American drama' and went on to praise him as director, actor, writer, designer 'and all-round genius'. It is likely that Welles himself wrote this part of the script. (*Author's collection*)

had done. Around eight, taking along two copies of the book, several pads of lined paper, a pair of scissors and handful of pencils and a paste pot, we moved over to Reuben's Restaurant two blocks away on 59th Street. While we worked we dined and then remained working after the table had been cleared – except for constantly renewed cups of coffee and cognac. By 10.30 p.m. we had got through the first section: the Count had just been observed crawling, batlike, down the sheer walls of his ancestral castle. Occasionally, an acquaintance passed by, paused for conversation and, receiving no encouragement, moved on.

As the after-theatre crowd began to arrive, we left the Carpathian Mountains with Count Dracula in a catatonic condition, safely nailed in his coffin and on his way, in a drifting abandoned coal scow, to England. By this time there was a pile of paste-stiffened paper on the edge of the table.

A Mercury secretary was called at home, where she was sleeping, and ordered to bring money to the restaurant to pay the bill. As soon as she left, Welles and Houseman ordered another meal and continued working. By 3 a.m. the place was empty again – not that either of them noticed. They were too busy dealing with Count Dracula, who by now had landed on a Cornish beach where, in the guise of a grey wolf, he had leapt ashore and vanished into the woods.

The restaurant boasted that it never closed and that night Welles and Houseman verified the claim as they continued to transfer Bram Stoker's horror story into an hour-long piece for radio actors. When cleaning staff arrived at the restaurant with pails, mops and brooms, they worked around the two men. After they had left, they ordered two large American breakfasts, and carried on working until 8 a.m. when they were finally ready to drive a burnt stake into the Count's heart before rising from the table. Three days later *Dracula* went on the air as the opening play of what was to become America's most legendary radio drama series.

The play opened with the CBS Symphony Orchestra playing the opening bars of Tchaikovsky's Piano Concerto No. 1 in B-flat minor, which became *The Mercury Theatre on the Air*'s regular signature tune. Announcer Dan Seymour, who introduced the programme for the rest of its run, told listeners, 'The Columbia Broadcasting Network is proud to present Orson Welles in a unique new summer series. In a single year, the first in the life of the Mercury Theatre, Orson Welles has come to be the most famous name of our time in American drama.' Quotes from newspapers and magazines praising Welles as a director, actor, writer, designer and all-round genius were read out. (It is likely that this part of the script was written by the Wonder Boy himself). Seymour told the audience that this was the first time a radio station had ever invited an entire theatre company onto the airwaves for a season.

The microphone was then given over to 'Orson Welles, the director of the Mercury Theatre, the star and producer of these programmes.' There was a pause before radio's best-known and most recognised voice bade the audience good evening followed by:

> The Mercury Theatre faces tonight a challenge and an opportunity for which we are grateful. During the next nine weeks we will present many different kinds of stories – stories of romance and adventure, biography, mystery and human emotion. Stories by authors like Robert Louis Stevenson, Emile Zola, Edgar Allan Poe, P. G. Wodehouse...

Welles then did something never done before in an American radio play – he generously introduced his leading players by name, telling the audience about the roles they had played at the Mercury Theatre. He would do something similar in the closing credits of his first film, *Citizen Kane*, two years later.

The live studio orchestra then began playing a piece of deeply mysterious music, under which can be heard the sound of a single bell tolling in the night. Over the music, Seymour informed the audience, '*The Mercury Theatre on the Air* presents Orson Welles as Count Dracula in his own version of Bram Stoker's great novel – *Dracula*!' Houseman's name and his part in adapting the book were not mentioned.

And so the drama unfolded, skilfully creating vivid pictures in the minds of its listeners. At the end, the atmospheric music was heard again and Dan Seymour returned to the microphone:

SEYMOUR: Tonight's production of Dracula by Orson Welles and the Mercury Theatre was the first of nine CBS broadcasts in which this brilliant group will bring to life a series of great narratives all presented in the immediacy of the first person singular. In presenting them each Monday evening in the summer season, the Columbia network is bringing an entire theatrical producing company to the air for the first time. And now here is the director to tell you about next week's thrilling production – Mr Orson Welles.

WELLES: Ladies and gentlemen, what are your favourite stories? If there is one you're particularly fond of and would like to hear on the air, will you please write me about it? Next week the Mercury Theatre is going to tell you Robert Louis Stevenson's exciting yarn about pirates and the sea, *Treasure Island*. Until then, in case Count Dracula has left you a little apprehensive, one word of comfort – when you go to bed tonight, don't worry, put out the lights and go to sleep. [Sound effect of a wolf howling to the moon.] Don't worry, that's just a sound effect. Over there in the shadows, see... Nothing! Nothing at all. Well, I think it's nothing. But always remember, ladies and gentlemen, there are wolves, there are vampires, such things do exist...

And Tchaikovsky's theme brought the evening to a close.

Audience figures for the Mercury's first radio production were disappointing, probably because there had been little time for CBS publicity staff to get sufficient advance promotional material out to newspapers and radio listings magazines. Programme and cast, however, were praised in newspapers the following morning day. Critics praised the actors for their intelligently acted, brilliantly conceived and highly entertaining show.

The weekly dramatisations were mapped out several days before each broadcast with *Treasure Island* becoming the second Monday play, followed by *A Tale of Two Cities*, *The Thirty-Nine Steps*, *Abraham Lincoln* and *The Count of Monte Cristo*. To write the scripts, Houseman decided to remain at home, sitting up in bed for up to fifteen hours each day to draft the fifty-seven-minute-long scripts used during the first series. On completion, he handed scripts to Welles for comment. Welles usually accepted them with minor corrections but, every once in a while, out of caprice or ego, or because he really felt he had a superior idea, he would make radical changes, for better or worse, before or during rehearsal.

Following the first programme and to ensure that Welles and his actors planned no surprises that might bring CBS into disrepute, Paley appointed network executive Davidson Taylor to oversee the Mercury's radio operations. Taylor was instructed to keep a close eye on the Mercury troupe and report back with information about their behavior, progress and – most importantly – ratings. He was, in effect, a spy in the camp – and everyone working on the show knew it.

Taylor's first job was to appoint an associate producer for the series; someone capable of keeping Welles in check, hold everything together and make sure that everything ran smoothly. The job went to Paul Stewart, the man who had given Welles one of his first radio jobs. After *Dracula* had been aired, Stewart heard rumours that Welles planned to produce the rest of the series himself. Stewart knew that Welles needed a good right-hand man in the studio to cover for his lack of experience and offered his services. Taylor paid him $85 per week – 'an extraordinary amount of money in those days,' Stewart later remembered – to organise rehearsals, run-throughs, music, effects and act as main liaison between CBS and the Mercury Theatre.

Rehearsals took place at the CBS studios every Wednesday, with Stewart reading the role Welles would eventually perform on the following Monday's live show. This was not because Welles thought it beneath his standing as radio's leading actor to attend mere rehearsals, but because he was simply too

Standing on a raised podium in front of a microphone and wearing headphones allowing him to hear everything and everyone – including himself – Welles 'conducted' his actors, waving his arms in the air to cue every spoken line, piece of music or sound effect. (*Library of Congress*)

busy directing at the Mercury Theatre, appearing in matinee performances, or acting in radio productions. Stewart arranged for rehearsals to be recorded onto wax discs, which were sent to Welles to play on a gramophone. He would then make final script adjustments or write notes to actors.

Welles only joined the cast on the day the show went out live, arriving at noon and throwing everything into disorder. Standing on a raised podium in front of a microphone and wearing headphones allowing him to hear everything and everyone – including himself – he 'conducted' his actors, waving his arms in the air to cue every spoken line, piece of music or sound effect.

Paul Stewart later recalled that final rehearsals were chaotic affairs because Welles 'was a very destructive man who had to destroy everything and then put it back together again himself. There were endless passionate discussions between him, Houseman and me. And then someone would say, "We're on the air in two minutes." The floor was strewn with paper. That we got on the air at all was a weekly miracle, because it was always like that.'

Houseman remembered, 'Shows were created week after week under conditions of soul- and health-destroying pressure.' On live broadcast days the cast, orchestra, sound effects and production team arrived in the studio in the early afternoon 'when two simultaneous dramas were regularly unfolded in the stale, tense air of Studio Number One: the minor drama of the current show and the major drama of Orson's gargantuan struggle to get it on. Sweating, howling, disheveled and single-handed he wrestled with chaos and time – always conveying an effect of being alone, traduced by his collaborators, surrounded by treachery, ignorance, sloth, indifference, incompetence and – more often than not – downright sabotage.'

Every week it was touch and go. As the hands of the clock moved relentlessly towards airtime, the crises grew more extreme, the perils more desperate. Often violence broke out. Scripts flew through the air, doors were slammed, batons snapped. At six – but usually nearer seven – there was a full run-through, a thing of wild improvisations and irrevocable disaster. One show was found to be twenty-one minutes too long, another fourteen and a half minutes too short.

With just minutes to go, there was a final frenzy of correction and reparation, of utter confusion and absolute horror, aggravated by the gulping down of sandwiches and bolting of oversized milkshakes. And then it was less than a minute to airtime…

'At that instant, quite regularly week after week – with not one second to spare – the titanic buffoonery stopped,' Houseman remembered. 'Suddenly out of the chaos, the show emerged – delicately poised, meticulously executed, precise as clockwork and smooth as satin. And above us all, like a rainbow over storm clouds, stood Orson on his podium, sonorous and heroic, a leader of men surrounded by his band of loyal followers; a giant in action, serene and radiant with the joy of a hard battle bravely fought – a great victory snatched from the jaws of disaster.'

# CHAPTER SIX

# Tempers, Tantrums and Men from Mars

*'It was an experience lasting six months I wouldn't have missed for the world*
*– nor would want to go through again.'*
*—Howard Koch*

*The Mercury Theatre on the Air*'s first nine Monday evening shows attracted a loyal following of around 5.5 million listeners – a disappointing audience for a nationwide, coast-to-coast programme and not enough to attract a sponsor prepared to bankroll a second series. Although Paley had found the broadcasts 'highbrow', he wanted CBS to be seen as a network offering something different from the others and he ordered Davidson Taylor to commission a further thirteen shows from Welles and Houseman. However, he warned that if a sponsor was not forthcoming by the end of the series in December 1938, it would be curtains for *The Mercury Theatre on the Air*.

Following a two-week break in September 1938, CBS decided to switch the show's broadcast day from Monday to Sunday evening. The network hoped the new broadcast day and series might attract a larger audience, arguing that a quality Sunday evening show might have more appeal to family audiences looking for a nice way to round off their weekend – a sort of bedtime story for people of all ages.

But by moving the show to a primetime Sunday evening slot, CBS was taking a huge gamble. For the last eleven months a skilled radio ventriloquist called Edgar Bergen and his wisecracking wooden dummy, Charley McCarthy, had dominated Sunday evening primetime radio with a programme on the NBC network, *The Chase and Sanborn Hour*. Chase & Sanborn Coffee, which sponsored the show, was delighted with the huge audiences Bergen and McCarthy attracted every week at 8 p.m. EST. In 1938, the show was said to 'have the ear of one-third of the nation and the largest radio audience in the United States'.

However, *The Chase and Sanborn Hour*, with its smooth MC, Don Ameche, guests from the world of movies, vaudeville and radio, cleverly written sketches, musical interludes and interruptions by the precocious wooden hero

Don Ameche was one of America's top radio stars in the 1930s and hosted *The Chase and Sanborn Hour*. He later became an Oscar-winning film actor, and made his final appearance in *Corrina, Corrina* just before his death in 1993. (*20th Century Fox Film Corporation*)

Charlie McCarthy – described as 'a debonair, girl-crazy, child-about-town – and a wooden one at that' – was not to everyone's taste.

Some found Bergen's dummy unfunny and often crude. In December 1937, Hollywood actress Mae West – who once said that 'too much of a good thing can be wonderful' and was famously known for her daring double entendres – was a guest on the show. As usual, Charlie McCarthy flirted with his female guest star and Mae West responded with her usual mixture of wit and risqué sexual references. Here is a flavour of the exchange between radio's wooden dummy and Hollywood's number one sex siren of the 1930s. The dialogue is tame compared with what is heard – and seen – on radio and TV today, but in 1937, the following dialogue was considered scandalous for Sunday evening family listening:

MCCARTHY: Could you even like Mr Bergen?

WEST: Ah, Mr Bergen. He's very sweet. In fact, he's a right guy. Confidentially, you'll have to show me a man I don't like.

MCCARTHY: That's swell! Bergen's your man. You know, he can be had.

WEST: On second thought, I'm liable to take him away from you.

MCCARTHY: Well, if you take Bergen away, I'm speechless.

WEST: Why don't you come up... Uh, home with me now, honey? I'll let you play in my woodpile.

In 1938, NBC's *The Chase and Sanborn Hour*, starring ventriloquist Edgar Bergen and dummy Charlie McCarthy, 'had the ear of one-third of the nation and the largest radio audience in the United States'. CBS decided to pit *The Mercury Theatre on the Air* against this popular Sunday evening show. (*Author's collection*)

MCCARTHY: Well, I'm not feeling very well tonight. I've been feeling very nervous lately. I think I'm gonna have a nervous breakdown. Whoop! There I go.

WEST: So, good-time Charlie's gonna play hard to get? Well, you can't kid me. You're afraid of women. Your Casanova stuff is just a front, a false front.

MCCARTHY: Not so loud, Mae, not so loud! All my girlfriends are listening.

WEST: Oh, yeah! You're all wood and a yard long.

MCCARTHY: Yeah.

WEST: You weren't so nervous and backward when you came up to see me at my apartment. In fact, you didn't need any encouragement to kiss me.

MCCARTHY: Did I do that?

WEST: Why, you certainly did. I got marks to prove it. An' splinters, too.

In a sketch in which West and Don Ameche played Adam and Eve in the Garden of Eden, West said, 'Get me a big one... I feel like doin' a big apple.' Following the show, NBC received letters branding the show 'immoral' and 'obscene'. Women's clubs and religious groups accused Chase & Sanborn Coffee of 'prostituting' their services by permitting 'impurity [to] invade the airwaves'. The news media called the exchange between Charlie and Mae 'the sex appeal battle of the century'. The Federal Communications Commission deemed the broadcast 'vulgar and indecent and far below even the minimum standard which should control in the selection and production of broadcast programs'. NBC passed all blame for the incident on West and banned her – and all mentions of her name – from its stations. West would not perform on American network radio for another twelve years.

Pitting *The Mercury Theatre on the Air* against *The Chase and Sanborn Hour* was known in radio circles as placing a programme in a 'throwaway position', meaning that no advertiser would bother going up against American's most popular programme. Yet the gravitas that *The Mercury Theatre on the Air* brought to the airwaves served to further Paley's image of CBS as 'the more enlightened network'.

The Mercury's second drama series, starting on 11 September 1938, included adaptations of *Julius Caesar, Jane Eyre, Sherlock Holmes, Oliver Twist* and *Around the World in Eighty Days*. The season ended on 4 December with an adaptation of Thornton Wilder's *The Bridge of San Luis Rey*.

To remove the pressure of writing weekly scripts from his own shoulders, Houseman engaged the services of a thirty-six-year-old 'earnest, spindly, 6-foot-2' New York-born lawyer turned playwright called Howard Koch to write the second series. By 1938 Koch had already had three plays produced in New York, although none ran for long or earned him much money. The chance to write for the Mercury Theatre for a few months earned him only $75 a week – but it would be a regular salary and was guaranteed. Koch later

Howard Koch, author of *The Mercury Theatre on the Air*'s production of *The War of the Worlds*. (*Peter Koch and the Koch family*)

admitted that his spell as a dramatist working for Welles and Houseman 'was an experience lasting six months I wouldn't have missed for the world – nor would want to go through again'.

Koch was contracted to write sixty pages of script to be ready by rehearsal time each week. To achieve this he was expected to work day and night. Both Welles and Houseman considered sleep a luxury that, for the most part, they denied themselves as well as their actors – and now their writer was also expected to follow suit.

Describing the way he was expected to write for *The Mercury Theatre on the Air*, Koch recalled,

> Early morning until late at night my pencil sped and, as energies dwindled, crawled over the yellow pages of my pad to be transcribed by the young college-girl-of-all-work who somehow learned to read my scrawl. Each batch of between fifteen or twenty pages would be rushed over to Welles and Houseman for their criticism and suggestions. Then came the revisions, and the revisions of the revisions *ad infinitum* until the deadline Sunday noon when Orson took over at rehearsals and worked his particular magic. The Girl Friday and I used to ponder how our two bosses were apparently thriving on this strenuous regime, gaining weight while the pounds were oozing off us. And for my part in all this I received the lordly sum of $75 a week. Only later did I realize that the fringe benefits of training and discipline were worth many times my salary.

It was Orson Welles' idea to dramatise H. G. Wells' 1897 story of an alien invasion of Earth, *The War of the Worlds*, into a radio play. Houseman sought permission from the British author's New York literary representative, Jacques Chambrun, to dramatise the story – failing to mention that the location and historical setting of the original would be changed from England in the early years of the twentieth century to New York in October 1939 – one year after the actual date of the broadcast.

Wells' original story had been published as a serial in the English magazine *Pearson's Weekly*, and in the United States in *The Cosmopolitan*. The story appeared in book form the following year, became an immediate bestseller on both sides of the Atlantic, was reprinted several times the same year, and has never been out of print since.

H. G. Wells' *The War of the Worlds* was set in a future still recognisable as Victorian England. It opens with the narrator, an author of scientific articles (like H. G. Wells himself), visiting an observatory in Ottershaw, a small Surrey town close to Wells' home, a small semi-detached house in Maybury Road on the outskirts of Woking. While Wells lived here, his novel *The Time Machine* was published and both *The War of the Worlds* and *The Invisible Man* were written.

At the observatory, where a 'well-known astronomer' worked, the narrator looks through the telescope and witnesses an explosion on the surface of the

'They cut every telegraph and wrecked the railways.' One of Warwick Goble's illustrations accompanying the 1897 serialisation of *The War of the Worlds* in *Pearson's Weekly* (Britain) and *The Cosmopolitan* (USA).

planet Mars, one of a series of galactic events that has been exciting English scientists. Later, a 'meteor' crashes on Horsell Common, a site well-known to Wells. The narrator is one of the first to discover that the 'meteor,' half-buried in an enormous pit created from the impact of the crash, is actually a space cylinder, thirty yards in diameter and caked in a thick, scaly layer of crust. To the horror of 300 onlookers, sounds begins emerging from the cylinder and a circular doorway in the side begins turning, disgorging snake-like tentacles followed by a hideous body, about the size of a large bear.

The creatures begin assembling some strange machinery in the crater. There is a flash of light and a pillar of green smoke rises into the air, engulfing the crowd. The smoke erupts into flames, incinerating the onlookers. Their blackened bodies are burnt to a crisp.

After returning home, the narrator witnesses what the Martians have been assembling: towering, three-legged 'fighting-machines' armed with Heat-Rays and chemical weapons. The machines smash through army units now positioned around the crater and attack surrounding communities. The narrator encounters a retreating artilleryman, who warns him that other cylinders have crash-landed in the district. The men attempt to escape together, but are separated during a Martian attack on the riverside town of Shepperton. More cylinders land across England and a frantic mass evacuation of London begins while the aliens destroy the capital.

After many hair-raising adventures, the narrator makes his way to a deserted London where he discovers that the alien invaders are dead, having succumbed to 'the putrefactive and disease bacteria against which their systems were unprepared; slain ... by the humblest things that God, in his wisdom, has put upon the earth'.

Following the 23 October broadcast of Jules Verne's *Around the World in Eighty Days*, Koch was handed a copy of H. G. Wells' novel with instructions from Houseman to be 'creative' with the storyline. Instead of placing the story in its original English setting of forty years previously, Koch was told that Welles wanted to relocate the scene to twentieth century America – on 30 October 1939 to be precise, exactly one year hence. Welles wanted Koch to give the script 'a realistic and first person singular feel' with actors playing the parts of on-the-spot reporters and eyewitnesses describing an alien attack on America in general – and New York in particular – via 'flash' news bulletins. Koch was reminded that the show would go out the night before Halloween, a time of the year in America long associated with pranks, jokes and fun…

Koch returned to his apartment on 72nd Street and began reading H. G. Wells' text. He quickly realised that he could use little apart from the original author's ideas of a Martian invasion and his description of their appearance and their death machines. From this, he was expected to write an hour-long play. That night Koch returned to bed in despair.

The following day was normally Koch's day off, but he decided to call Houseman to see if *The War of the Worlds* could be postponed. From the sound of Koch's voice, Houseman knew that his writer was in a panic,

The Martians land in Surrey in a drawing by Frank R. Paul for the publication of H. G. Wells' *The War of the Worlds* in *Amazing Stories* in 1927. (© *Experimenter Publishing* Co.)

'pleading to have the assignment changed to another subject'. Houseman said he would speak to Welles. When the telephone rang moments later, the worried dramatist rushed to answer. 'The answer is a firm "no",' said Houseman. 'This is Orson's favourite project. Get on with it.'

Koch decided to clear his head and drive out of the city for a few hours to visit his family in Kingston, NY, all the while thinking of a credible way to tell the story of the Martian invasion of America. On the journey back it occurred to him that if the aliens were to land in America he needed a map to select a location for the first Martian arrivals. He pulled into a gas station and, since he was on Route 9W where it crosses through part of New Jersey, the attendant gave him a map of the state.

Back in New York and feeling refreshed, he went to work, spreading out the map and looking for a suitable place to invade from outer space. His eyes fell on a tiny community called Grover's Mill, part of the township of West Windsor, near the capital of New Jersey, Trenton. He liked the sound of Grover's Mill; it had an authentic ring and was a real place, although Koch had never visited the community and had no time to pay a courtesy call before the play went on the air. It was also near Princeton, where he could logically bring in the observatory that would first notice strange things happening on Mars.

But Houseman later recalled that after three days of slaving trying to Americanise H. G. Wells' sci-fi fantasy, Koch was again ready to give up. He found it almost impossible to make the story interesting or in any way credible to modern American ears. 'Koch was not given to habitual alarmism,' said Houseman. 'To confirm this Annie, our secretary, came to the telephone. "You can't do it!" she whined. "Those old Martians are just a load of nonsense. It's all too silly! We're going to make fools of ourselves. Absolute fools!"'

There was one possible alternative for the Sunday play, now just a few days away, in an adaptation of the novel *Lorna Doone*. Houseman again tried to reach Welles by telephone, but he was too busy rehearsing and had insisted on no interruptions. 'The reason he wouldn't come to the 'phone was that he was in his thirty-sixth successive hour of rehearsing *Danton's Death*, a play by Georg Büchner out of which Max Reinhardt had made a mass spectacle in the 1920s,' said Houseman. 'Not to be outdone, Orson had glued 1,700 masks to the back wall of the Mercury Theatre and ripped out the entire stage.'

Unable to talk to Welles, Houseman called Koch back. His tone was severe and he accused the writer of defeatism. He offered to come over and help, but when he arrived at Koch's apartment at 2 a.m. the following morning, things were looking better. 'He was having fun laying waste to the state of New Jersey,' remembered Houseman. Together Houseman and Koch revised the script and cut out speaking roles for four female characters – turning it into an all-male piece – thus eliminating a role for Agnes Moorehead, one of the Mercury's most critically acclaimed actresses. 'We worked all night and through the next day. At sunset the script was finished,' said Houseman.

It was Welles' idea to dramatise *The War of the Worlds* for radio, but the script was written by Howard Koch, a thirty-six-year-old former lawyer turned playwright seen here working on the script. (*Screenwriters' Guild of America*)

On Thursday 27 October, Paul Stewart called a read-through and a rehearsal that was, as usual, recorded for Welles to listen to whenever he had a moment free from *Danton's Death*. The cast listened to the recording before going home. They left after midnight feeling gloomy. They felt they had the radio equivalent of a theatrical 'turkey' on their hands unless something could be done quickly to save the situation.

Houseman personally took the recording to Welles' room at the St Regis Hotel, where he was staying until the upcoming production of *Danton's Death* had completed its run. Welles arrived at the hotel exhausted, following a full day of rehearsals. During the early hours of the morning he listened to the recording with Houseman and agreed that it was, indeed, a dull show. 'We felt that its only chance of coming off lay in emphasising its newscast style – its simultaneous eyewitness quality,' remembered Houseman.

Welles and Houseman spent the rest of the night spicing up the script with circumstantial allusions and authentic detail and later that day the script was sent across to CBS to be approved by the network censor. Under protest and with a deep sense of grievance, they made twenty-seven minor changes insisted on by the censors, including changing the name of the Hotel Biltmore to a non-existent Park Plaza and the CBS Building to 'the broadcasting building'.

The script then went to the typing pool, where a final version was produced and copies were made ready for the broadcast. 'And then we went to bed,' said Houseman. 'We had done our best and, after all, a show is just a show.'

Saturday 29 October was the day before the broadcast and Paul Stewart rehearsed the cast with the CBS sound effects team. CBS was famous for the realistic effects used on its radio shows, which stretched from comedy explosions to doors eerily creaking open, the sound of an army on the march and an owl hooting in the night.

Unique and highly realistic effects were created for *The Mercury Theatre on the Air*, including the sound of a wooden ship plying its way through choppy waters to a distant island – complete with creaking decks and wind in the sails – a lone wolf howling at the moon while greeting Count Dracula, a head being removed from the rest of its body by a guillotine blade, and the wheels of a carriage bouncing off the wet cobbles of London's foggy streets. When *The Count of Monte Cristo* went on air, a pair of actors in a dungeon scene had to lie on the stone floor of the men's room and deliver their lines through a special dynamic microphone set at the base of the toilet seat to achieve the correct 'echo sound' of a stone prison. A second microphone was placed inside a toilet bowl at the other end of the building and was constantly flushed to give a faithful rendering of waves breaking against prison walls.

A remarkable lady called Ora Nichols headed the CBS sound effects department. Ora was not simply a highly talented sound effects engineer, but by 1938 had also broken social boundaries by becoming the first woman to be placed in charge of radio sound effects. In 1938, she remained the only woman with such a role. Her abilities earned the respect and attention of everyone who was anyone in the medium and she was once voted 'the most influential woman in radio'.

Ora had begun her career working behind the scenes in vaudeville and silent films before entering the world of radio. She had originally trained as a musician, but found sound effects more fascinating. She became famous for her thrilling effects work on the *Buck Rogers* radio shows and she brought fascinating new sounds to the airwaves, including using an electric shaver and an air conditioning vent to create the sound of Buck's rocket ship.

With her colleagues James Rogan and Ray Kremer, Ora's brilliant contributions to *The War of the Worlds* would include chilling sounds of a Martian cylinder unscrewing, bomber planes flying and a dying New York City under a Martian gas attack.

Ora's team had only a few days each week to develop new effects that would fit the needs of a different weekly script and the demands of Orson Welles. All effects were relayed 'live' and the trio would spend hours inventing complex new devices for *The Mercury Theatre on the Air*, such as using a pneumatic device to simulate machine-gun fire, dropping timpani hammers onto a huge drum for the sound a Martian spaceship vibrating and sliding one iron panel over another across the floor of an echo chamber to create the impression of metal spaceship doors opening and closing.

The effects team also helped young Frank Readick, who played the role of a roving radio reporter, to describe the scene when the Martian meteorite opens to reveal the leathery tentacles and terrible, pale-eyed faces of the creatures inside. The team suggested that Readick listen to the famous recording made by WLS Chicago radio reporter Herb Morrison describing the exploding of the airship *Hindenburg* at Lakehurst the previous year. Morrison's is a classic piece of on-the-spot recording, one of those incredible, unpredictable accidents of eyewitness description. The reporter was casually describing a routine landing of the giant airship and then, after a flash of flame, he witnessed the whole thing exploding into the night sky. Writhing human figures twisted and squirmed as they fell from the burning wreckage to his cry of 'Oh, the humanity…'

Readick was allowed to take the recoding home, where he played it over and over again to allow him to recreate Morrison's emotions in his own terms as he prepared to describe the meteorite dramatically coming to life.

As well as the realistic sound effects, music played an important part in the Mercury's radio productions. Out of an hour's playing time it was not unusual to have thirty or forty minutes of music to introduce and end the show, link scenes, and play quietly in the background. In the theatre, Welles and Houseman relied upon the composing and piano-playing talent of Marc Blitzstein for musical scores and accompaniment, but as part of the CBS contract they were obliged to use the CBS Symphony Orchestra under the baton of twenty-seven-year-old Bernard Herrmann, who Houseman named 'the golden boy of radio around CBS'. The orchestra could either be used in its entirety or be broken down into smaller units for Sunday broadcasts.

New York-born Herrmann – 'Benny' to his friends – was a serious musician and not always pleased to conduct what he considered second-rate music for radio shows. Houseman remembered him as 'egotistical, contentious, devoted, enormously well-read, he managed then – and later – to combine a serious musical career with work for the mass media'.

His first major success was to be hired in 1934 by CBS, for whom he wrote incidental music to accompany educational programmes and conducted the resident symphony orchestra. This lead to his being asked to write music for radio drama, a role he made his own. His music transformed a static medium into something worthy of attention. It was Herrmann's idea to begin each Sunday show with the opening bars of Tchaikovsky's Piano Concerto No. 1 in B-flat Minor, which became its signature tune.

Herrmann was happy to provide 'classical style' music to dramas, but when Welles told him that the early part of *The War of the Worlds* required the music of a dance band, the maestro was horrified.

Paul Stewart remembered: 'CBS would not give us a dance band on this occasion so we had to use the symphony men and getting Benny to perform the kind of music I had in mind was almost an impossibility. He didn't understand the rhythms or anything. I remember saying to him, "Benny, it's gotta be a beat like this…" And I snapped my fingers, which made him very upset. He handed me the baton and said, "You conduct it!" So I got up on his little podium and all the musicians looked at me. They all understood his personality, so when I gave the downbeat, they played it just the way I wanted it. I handed the baton back to Benny and he was crestfallen.'

Stewart claims that he 'never saw Benny happy'. He recalled, 'He always seemed very impatient and it was his impatience and apparent lack of humour that made him the butt of many jokes by Welles and Houseman; he was teased a lot to show this side of his personality. The orchestra did it more than anybody. They were so pleased that time when I took his baton.'

Rehearsals for the Sunday shows were often dramas in themselves. Said Stewart, 'There would be frantic fights to the last second to get the programmes on the air. Between Welles, Houseman and myself there would be script pages crossed out – and we'd always have to cut Benny down, too.'

The problem was that some script changes failed to be passed onto Herrmann, meaning that sometimes music was played when it was not expected – or not played at all when actors expected a musical cue. Afterwards Herrmann would storm at Stewart, 'Why didn't ya tell me? How can I do this?'

'Everybody admired Herrmann,' said Stewart, 'but they found him a little difficult, which is true of all artists. Particularly when presenting live radio. Time was of the essence and there simply wasn't time to waste on temperamental people.'

The entire cast of *The War of the Worlds* – including Orson Welles – thought that the play was destined to become the radio equivalent of a theatrical 'turkey'. (*Author's collection*)

The relationship between Herrmann and Welles was tempestuous – yet highly productive. Amid screaming rows, the snapping of batons, accusations of sabotage (by both parties) and scripts and scores hurled into the air – and at each other – they understood one another perfectly.

\* \* \*

On the same day that *The War of the Worlds* was to go on air, *The New York Times* carried an article headlined 'Radio Challenges Playwrights to Try New Tricks'. The piece was based on an interview with Welles' friend Archibald MacLeish, in which the Pulitzer Prize-winning writer urged producers of American radio drama to 'try new tricks' to make programmes more realistic. MacLeish had set an example a few days before with the broadcast of his realistic verse play *Air Raid*.

Alongside a photograph of Welles rehearsing the Mercury company, the article likened a radio play to an air raid:

> The terror will last for thirty minutes. The American radio audience has never had such a horrifying experience, and so the problem of the dramatist becomes more acute. He must make it sound real. His is the trick of plucking on the strings of imagination to bring out the story just as the composer patterns a symphony. Thematic sounds must be woven through the fabric of the tale.
>
> Sirens screech. The populace in noisy confusion runs to shelter. Bombers hum in the distance, but in no time they soar overhead with a deafening buzz. Machine guns splutter. Anti-aircraft guns boom. Bombs explode and buildings crumble. The terror over, the dull drone of the vanishing enemy planes mixes with the agonizing cries of the people and in thirty minutes the show is over on the air. It took six months to write and several weeks to produce and long hours of rehearsal. A symphonic masterpiece or tone poem can be broadcast over and over again, but not so with a drama, be it poetic or prose. That's what radio offers the playwright.

Perhaps MacLeish had failed to tune into *The Mercury Theatre on the Air* and had not heard its truthful acting and imaginative sounds effects for himself? Is it possible he had failed to hear about the ability of his friends Welles and Houseman to churn out hour-long shows week after week? Had he not read positive reviews of the company's work in all the best newspapers?

All Archibald MacLeish had to do to experience a truly horrifying experience coupled with realistic sound effects reflecting death and destruction was to reach for his radio and tune into the CBS network at 8 p.m. that very evening.

*The War of the Worlds* was about to go on the air…

CHAPTER SEVEN

# Mars Attacks!

*'We have learned now that we cannot regard this planet as being fenced in and a secure abiding place for Man; we can never anticipate the unseen good or evil that may come upon us suddenly out of space.'*
—H. G. Wells, The War of the Worlds, *1898*

A large group of actors and technicians moved into the CBS studio during the early afternoon of 30 October. Technicians and producers sat in the control room, which was separated from the studio by a large soundproofed glass wall, behind which stood the actors, orchestra and their conductor.

Present were Houseman and Stewart (who would also be playing two small parts in the play), plus actors for that evening's show including Dan Seymour (the announcer), Frank Readick, Ray Collins, Carl Frank, Kenny Delmar, Richard Wilson, William Alland, Stefan Schnabel, William Herz and Howard Smith. Some of the actors would play two, three or four different roles in the play.

Also in the control room was Davidson Taylor – always around to keep a watchful eye on Welles and ever ready to report back to his boss, William S. Paley – and WABC sound engineer John Dietz. Bernard Herrmann and members of the CBS Symphony Orchestra went through to the soundproofed studio, along with the sound effects trio of Ora Nichols, Ray Kremer and Jim Rogan.

Last to arrive was Welles, who had rushed to the studio from the theatre where he was still rehearsing *Danton's Death* for all it was worth. Now the run-through could begin.

Halfway through the run-through, Richard Wilson (playing three parts in the play) recalled that at one stage Welles dropped his script to the side of his body and remarked, 'This is the worst piece of crap I've ever had to do.' The entire cast, including Welles, the crew and the orchestra, broke into laughter, probably because none of them really believed in the piece or its ability to take an audience by surprise.

As the cast took a short break before returning for the live broadcast, Welles asked a sound engineer what he thought of the show. 'Put it this way, it's not one of your better ones,' said the technician. 'It's dull, very dull.'

'What don't you like about it?' asked Welles.

'It'll put them to sleep,' said the technician. 'There's no human interest, no love interest.'

The cast and crew returned to the studio shortly afterwards, feeling downcast. It was too late to do anything about it. The great American public was expecting to hear *The War of the Worlds* and that's what they would be getting – for better or worse.

Five seconds before the play went live, sound engineer John Dietz began the countdown: 'Five, four, three, two, one – you're on the air.'

This was the cue for announcer Dan Seymour to step up to the microphone and tell listeners, 'The Columbia Broadcasting System and its affiliated stations present Orson Welles and *The Mercury Theatre on the Air* in *The War of the Worlds* by H. G. Wells...'

This was Bernard Herrmann's cue to raise his baton. The orchestra began playing the opening bars of the Mercury's signature theme. Over the music, Seymour added, 'Ladies and gentlemen: the director of the Mercury Theatre and star of these broadcasts, Orson Welles...'

Welles then began to speak Howard Koch's version of H. G. Wells' own opening passage from *The War of the Worlds* – with the date clearly stating that the setting was taking place 'in the early years of the twentieth century'.

*The Mercury Theatre on the Air* in rehearsal. Orson Welles conducts the actors, Bernard Herrmann handles the musicians. (© *Bettmann/CORBIS*)

We know now that in the early years of the twentieth century this world was being watched closely by intelligences greater than man's and yet as mortal as his own. We know now that as human beings busied themselves about their various concerns they were scrutinized and studied, perhaps almost as narrowly as a man with a microscope might scrutinize the transient creatures that swarm and multiply in a drop of water. With infinite complacence people went to and fro over the earth about their little affairs, serene in the assurance of their dominion over this small spinning fragment of solar driftwood which by chance or design man has inherited out of the dark mystery of Time and Space. Yet across an immense ethereal gulf, minds that are to our minds as ours are to the beasts in the jungle, intellects vast, cool and unsympathetic regarded this earth with envious eyes and slowly and surely drew their plans against us.

Audience members listening carefully would then have heard Welles hint that the story about to take place was set in the future and not the present: 'In the *thirty-ninth* year of the twentieth century came the great disillusionment...' He continued:

It was near the end of October. Business was better. The war scare was over. More men were back at work. Sales were picking up. On this particular evening, 30 October, the Crossley service estimated that 32 million people were listening in on radios...

* * *

A radio announcer reads out a weather report before announcing that the station is now going over to the Meridian Room in the Hotel Park Plaza in downtown New York, where audiences are to be entertained by the music of Ramón Raquello and his orchestra.

A Spanish tango is heard and the announcer informs the audience that Ramón Raquello's orchestra will now play *La Cumparsita*. Three minutes and thirty-eight seconds into the programme, the announcer is back at the microphone telling the audience that he is interrupting the music 'to bring a special bulletin from the Intercontinental Radio News. At twenty minutes before eight, central time, Professor Farrell of the Mount Jennings Observatory, Chicago, Illinois, reports observing several explosions of incandescent gas, occurring at regular intervals on the planet Mars.' He adds that the spectroscope indicates the gas to be hydrogen 'moving towards the Earth with enormous velocity'. He says that Professor Pierson of Princeton Observatory confirms Farrell's observation, and describes the phenomenon as 'like a jet of blue flame shot from a gun'.

The audience is then taken back to the music of Ramón Raquello just as the piece is coming to an end. Applause can be heard from an audience.

The announcer introduces 'a tune that never loses favour, the ever-popular "Star Dust"' and Ramón Raquello's orchestra begins playing Hoagy Carmichael's timeless classic. Seconds later, however, he is back with another newsflash, which states that the government's Meteorological Bureau has requested the country's observatories to keep astronomical watch on any further disturbances occurring on the planet Mars. 'Due to the unusual nature of this occurrence, we have arranged an interview with noted astronomer, Professor Pierson, who will give us his views on the event. In a few moments we will take you to the Princeton Observatory at Princeton, New Jersey. We return you until then to the music of Ramón Raquello and his orchestra.

Following a few bars from Mr Raquello, the announcer states that the station is ready to go over to the Princeton Observatory, where reporter Carl Phillips (played by Frank Readick) will interview Professor Richard Pierson (Orson Welles), the famous astronomer.

Six minutes into the programme, the scene switches to the observatory. A ticking noise echoes and the excited reporter reveals that he is standing in a large semicircular room, pitch black except for an oblong split in the ceiling. 'Through this opening I can see a sprinkling of stars that cast a kind of frosty glow over the intricate mechanism of the huge telescope. The ticking sound you hear is the vibration of the clockwork. Professor Pierson stands directly above me on a small platform, peering through a giant lens. I ask you to be patient, ladies and gentlemen, during any delay that may arise during our interview. Besides his ceaseless watch of the heavens, Professor Pierson may be interrupted by telephone or other communications. During this period he is in constant touch with the astronomical centers of the world. Professor, may I begin our questions?'

The professor agrees and Phillips asks him to tell radio listeners exactly what he sees as he observes Mars through his telescope.

'Nothing unusual,' says the professor. 'A red disk swimming in a blue sea. Transverse stripes across the disk. Quite distinct now because Mars happens to be the point nearest the earth – in opposition, as we call it.'

Phillips asks what the transverse stripes signify and Pierson replies, 'Not canals, I can assure you, Mr Phillips, although that's the popular conjecture of those who imagine Mars to be inhabited. From a scientific viewpoint the stripes are merely the result of atmospheric conditions peculiar to the planet.'

The reporter asks if Pierson is 'quite convinced as a scientist that living intelligence as we know it does not exist on Mars?'

'I'd say the chances against it are a thousand to one,' replies Pierson.

Phillips asks how far Mars is from earth and is told that the planet is approximately 40 million miles away. 'Well, that seems a safe enough distance,' remarks the reporter. He is just about to close the interview when he tells the audience, 'Just a moment, ladies and gentlemen, someone has just handed Professor Pierson a message which he has just received. Professor, may I read the message to the listening audience?'

Pierson agrees and Phillips reads the message aloud, stating that it is a wire addressed to Professor Pierson from Dr Gray of the National History Museum, New York, 9.15 p.m. EST. Phillips continues that a seismograph had registered shock of almost earthquake intensity occurring within a radius of twenty miles of Princeton. 'Please investigate. Signed, Lloyd Gray, Chief of Astronomical Division.'

[Listeners who had heard the radio drama from the start would have taken little notice of references to the time of day. However, others just tuned into WABC might have been confused by mention of the time as 9.15 p.m. when it was, in fact, only eight minutes after eight.]

Phillips asks Pierson if the occurrence might possibly have something to do with the disturbances observed on the planet Mars. 'Hardly,' says Pierson. 'This is probably a meteorite of unusual size and its arrival at this particular time is merely a coincidence. However, we shall conduct a search, as soon as daylight permits.'

Phillips hands listeners back to the studio, from where piano music is heard.

\* \* \*

At the same time as *The Mercury Theatre on the Air* was transmitting *The War of the Worlds* live across the CBS network, in a radio theatre a mile away a large audience was enjoying *The Chase and Sanborn Hour*, starring Edgar Bergen and his wooden dummy Charlie McCarthy, Don Ameche, singer Nelson Eddy – star of the recent musical film *Naughty Marietta* – actress/singer Dorothy Lamour and British-born Hollywood star Madeleine Carroll. On that Sunday evening 34.7 per cent of all American radio listeners were tuned in to Charlie McCarthy and his human stooge and just 3.6 per cent to *The Mercury Theatre on the Air*.

Despite being America's favourite radio show, the NBC variety programme transmitted that night was hardly a vintage edition. The jokes cracked by Edgar Bergen and his dummy were lame and a pair of songs delivered by Nelson Eddy – 'The Vagabond Song' and 'The Canadian Loggers' Song' – caused thousands of listeners to twiddle their radio dials to see if anything better was on the air at the same time. As *The Chase and Sanborn Hour* progressed, things began to get worse. Eleven minutes into their show there was an interminable eight-minute-long sketch in which Bergen attempted to tell a ghost story while Charlie the dummy told Don Ameche and Nelson Eddy about the Halloween mischief he was planning. Things got a little better following a commercial for Chase & Sanborn coffee and fifteen minutes into the programme Dorothy Lamour arrived to sing Hoagy Carmichael's new song 'Two Sleepy People', followed by Don Ameche and Madeline Carroll in scenes from John Van Druten's play *There's Always Juliet*.

Miss Lamour sang well and Mr Ameche and Miss Carroll played with conviction, but tens of thousands of people across the country had done what they always did when they became disinterested in what they were tuned into. Years later, television viewers would do just the same by surfing through their channels hoping to find something more entertaining. And as they twiddled their radio dials away from *The Chase and Sanborn Hour*, they passed through classical music concerts and Sunday evening religious broadcasts before coming across an announcer urgently reading a news bulletin about a 'huge, flaming object, believed to be a meteorite, which fell on a farm in the neighbourhood of Grover's Mill, New Jersey, twenty-two miles from Trenton'. They heard him say that a flash in the night sky was visible within a radius of several hundred miles and that a special mobile unit was on its way to the scene, where reporter Carl Phillips was preparing to describe the scene to listeners as soon as he arrived from Princeton.

'In the meantime, we take you to the Hotel Martinet in Brooklyn, where Bobby Millette and his orchestra are offering a programme of dance music.'

Instead of tuning back to *The Chase and Sanborn Hour*, newly arrived listeners were intrigued by what they had just heard – or what they *thought* they had just heard. Something about a huge flaming object falling on a farm in New Jersey. Thousands decided to stay with the programme to discover what might happen – unaware they had tuned into a radio play…

\* \* \*

A swing band plays for twenty seconds before cutting out. We join Carl Phillips at Grover's Mill. 'Ladies and gentlemen, this is Carl Phillips again, at the Wilmuth Farm, Grover's Mill, New Jersey,' the reporter announces breathlessly. 'Professor Pierson and myself made the eleven miles from Princeton in ten minutes. Well, I hardly know where to begin, to paint for you a word picture of the strange scene before my eyes, like something out of a modern *Arabian Nights*. Well, I just got here. I haven't had a chance to look around yet. I guess that's it. Yes, I guess that's the… thing, directly in front of me, half buried in a vast pit. Must have struck with terrific force. The ground is covered with splinters of a tree it must have struck on its way down. What I can see of the object itself doesn't look very much like a meteor, at least not the meteors I've seen. It looks more like a huge cylinder. It has a diameter of… What would you say, Professor Pierson?'

The professor guesses around thirty yards.

Phillips says that the metal on the sheath is 'sort of yellowish-white'. He adds that curious spectators are pressing close to the object in spite of police efforts to hold them back. Mr Wilmuth, a local farmer (played by Ray Collins), is brought to the microphone and asked about 'this rather unusual visitor that dropped in your backyard'.

'Well, I was listenin' to the radio,' says Mr Wilmuth, 'I was kinda drowsin' and that Professor fellow was talkin' about Mars, so I was half dozin' and half listenin' to the radio kinda halfways… And I heard something. It was a hissing sound. Like this: sssssss… Kinda like a fourt' of July rocket. I turned my head out the window and would have swore I was to sleep and dreamin'.

I seen a kinda greenish streak and then zingo! Somethin' smacked the ground. Knocked me clear out of my chair!'

Phillips says that he wishes he could convey the atmosphere of this fantastic scene to the listeners. Hundreds of cars are parked in a field and police are roping off the roadway leading to the farm, but spectators are breaking through, eager to witness the scene for themselves. Vehicle headlights throw an enormous spot onto the pit where the object is half-buried. 'Some of the more daring souls are now venturing near the edge. Their silhouettes stand out against the metal sheen,' he reports.

A faint humming sound is heard – and the time has come for actor Frank Readick in his role as Carl Phillips to go into his *Hindenburg* mode and describe what he is witnessing in the Grover's Mill field. 'Now, ladies and gentlemen, there's something I haven't mentioned in all this excitement, but now it's becoming more distinct,' says Phillips. 'Perhaps you've caught it already on your radio. Listen.'

There is a long pause.

'Do you hear it?' continues the reporter. 'It's a curious humming sound that seems to come from inside the object. I'll move the microphone nearer. Now we're not more than 25 feet away. Can you hear it now? Professor Pierson – can you tell us the meaning of that scraping noise inside the thing?'

The professor answers that it is probably the unequal cooling of its surface. 'Do you still think it's a meteor, professor?' asks the reporter.

'I don't know what to think,' answers Pierson. 'The metal casing is definitely extraterrestrial... not found on this earth. Friction with the earth's atmosphere usually tears holes in a meteorite. This thing is smooth and, as you can see, of cylindrical shape...'

Phillips interrupts with a cry: 'Just a minute! Something's happening! Ladies and gentlemen, this is terrific! This end of the thing is beginning to flake off! The top is beginning to rotate like a screw! The thing must be hollow!'

Voices are heard in the crowd, saying, 'She's movin'! Look, the darn thing's unscrewing! Keep back, there! Keep back, I tell you! Maybe there's men in it trying to escape! It's red hot, they'll burn to a cinder! Keep back there. Keep those idiots back!'

The clanking sound of a huge piece of metal falling is heard.

Voices cry out. 'She's off! The top's loose! Look out there! Stand back...'

Phillips confesses that this is the most terrifying thing he has ever witnessed. 'Wait a minute! Someone's crawling out of the hollow top. Someone or... something. I can see peering out of that black hole two luminous disks... Are they eyes? It might be a face. It might be...'

There is a shout of awe from the crowd.

Phillips keeps the commentary going by saying, 'Good heavens, something's wriggling out of the shadow like a gray snake. Now it's another one, and another. They look like tentacles to me. There, I can see the thing's body. It's large, large as a bear and it glistens like wet leather. But that face, it... Ladies and gentlemen, it's indescribable. I can hardly force myself to keep looking at it. The eyes are black and gleam like a serpent. The mouth is v-shaped with saliva dripping from its rimless lips that seem to quiver and pulsate. The monster or whatever it is can hardly move. It seems weighed down by... possibly gravity or something. The thing's raising up. The crowd falls back now. They've seen plenty. This is the most extraordinary experience. I can't find words... I'll pull this microphone with me as I talk. I'll have to stop the description until I can take a new position. Hold on, will you please, I'll be right back in a minute...'

Seconds later Phillips is back. He tells listeners he is standing at the back of a stone wall that adjoins Mr Wilmuth's garden and from here gets a sweep of the whole scene. 'I'll give you every detail as long as I can talk. As long as I can see. More state police have arrived. They're drawing up a cordon in front of the pit, about thirty of them. No need to push the crowd back now. They're willing to keep their distance. The captain is conferring with someone. We can't quite see who. Oh yes, I believe it's Professor Pierson. Yes, it is. Now they've parted. The Professor moves around one side, studying the object, while the captain and two policemen advance with something in their hands. I can see it now. It's a white handkerchief tied to a pole... A flag of truce. If those creatures know what that means... what anything means...! Wait! Something's happening...!'

There is a fierce hissing sound followed by humming that increases in intensity. Phillips reports excitedly, 'A humped shape is rising out of the pit. I can make out a small beam of light against a mirror. What's that? There's a jet of flame springing from the mirror, and it leaps right at the advancing men. It strikes them head on! Good Lord, they're turning into flame...!'

There are screams and unearthly shrieks...

The whole field is now on fire. There is an explosion as trees, barns and the gas tanks of cars erupt. 'It's spreading everywhere, it's coming this way, about twenty yards to my right,' screams Phillips – and then listeners hear the sound of a microphone being dropped onto the ground – followed by dead silence.

Another announcer comes on air and explains, 'Due to circumstances beyond our control, we are unable to continue the broadcast from Grover's Mill. Evidently there's some difficulty with our field transmission. However, we will return to that point at the earliest opportunity... We now continue with our piano interlude.'

\* \* \*

The first telephone calls began coming into the CBS switchboard around eighteen minutes into the programme.

'Can you tell me, please, have Martians really landed in America?'

'Are we really being invaded by alien creatures from another planet?'

'What's really going on out at Grover's Mill? Have the Germans invaded America?'

'What's happened to that nice dance music we heard earlier on – it keeps going off while some guy bangs on about meteorites falling from outer space. Put the music back on…'

As the actors continued with their performances – and unbeknown to anyone inside the CBS studio – the New Jersey State Police were racing towards Grover's Mill. Elsewhere, people across the United States were praying, crying, frantically fleeing to escape death from alien invaders, telephoning friends and neighbours to warn them that doom and destruction were coming their way. Some called newspaper offices and hospitals, others summoned police cars. They said they had heard newsflashes on the radio, so it had to be true…

Meanwhile, the play continued with everyone in the studio blissfully unaware of what was happening outside of their little world of weekly radio drama.

\* \* \*

Over the WABC airwaves an announcer says that he has been handed a message from Grover's Mill by telephone. At least forty people, including six state troopers, lie dead in a field east of the village of Grover's Mill, their bodies burned and distorted beyond all possible recognition. The next voice is that of Brigadier General Montgomery Smith, commander of the state militia at Trenton, New Jersey.

Brigadier Smith (played by Richard Wilson) says that he has been requested by the governor of New Jersey to place the surrounding counties under martial law. No one is permitted to enter this area except by special pass issued by state or military authorities. Four companies of state militia are proceeding from Trenton to Grover's Mill, and will aid in the evacuation of homes within the range of military operations.

More details of the Grover's Mill catastrophe arrive. The strange creatures, after unleashing their deadly assault, have crawled back to their pit and are making no attempt to prevent firemen from recovering bodies and extinguishing flames. For the moment all contact with Carl Phillips and the mobile radio unit is lost.

Suddenly the announcer is back, speaking urgently. 'Ladies and gentlemen, I have just been informed that we have finally established communication with an eyewitness of the tragedy. Professor Pierson has been located at a farmhouse near Grover's Mill where he has established an emergency observation post. As a scientist, he will give you his explanation of the calamity. The next voice you hear will be that of Professor Pierson, brought to you by direct wire. Professor Pierson.'

The sound of microphone feedback is heard before Pierson tells listeners that he is unable to provide any authoritative information about the creatures in the rocket cylinder – neither their nature, their origin, nor their purposes here on Earth. 'Of their destructive instrument I might venture some conjectural explanation. For want of a better term, I shall refer to the mysterious weapon as a Heat-Ray. It's all too evident that these creatures have scientific knowledge far in advance of our own.'

He is interrupted by another newsflash from Trenton. It is a brief statement stating that the charred body of Carl Phillips has been identified in a Trenton hospital. Another bulletin from the director of the National Red Cross reports ten units of Red Cross emergency workers have been assigned to the headquarters of the state militia stationed outside Grover's Mill. A bulletin from police at Princeton Junction says that fires at Grover's Mill are now under control. Scouts report that all is quiet in the pit and no sign of life appears from the mouth of the cylinder. A special statement from Mr Harry McDonald, vice-president in charge of operations, follows.

Harry McDonald (played by Ray Collins) tells listeners that he has received a request from the Trenton militia to place at their disposal the network's entire broadcasting facilities. In view of the gravity of the situation, and believing that radio has a responsibility to serve the public interest at all times, the network is turning its facilities over to the state militia at Trenton.

The action switches to the field headquarters of the state militia near Grover's Mill, where Captain Lansing of the signal corps (played by Kenny Delmar) says, 'The situation arising from the reported presence of certain individuals of unidentified nature is now under complete control.' He adds that the cylindrical object lying in the pit directly below his position is surrounded by eight battalions of infantry armed with rifles and machine guns. 'All cause for alarm, if such cause ever existed, is now entirely unjustified,' he assures listeners. 'The things, whatever they are, do not even venture to poke their heads above the pit. I can see their hiding place plainly in the glare of the searchlights here. With all their reported resources, these creatures can scarcely stand up against heavy machine-gun fire. Anyway, it's an interesting outing for the troops.'

Lansing notices 'slight smoke in the woods bordering the Millstone River. Fire started by campers. Well, we ought to see some action soon. One of the companies is deploying on the left flank. A quick thrust and it will all be over.'

Suddenly he blurts out, 'Now wait a minute! I see something on top of the cylinder. No, it's nothing but a shadow. Now the troops are on the edge of the Wilmuth Farm. 7,000 armed men closing in on an old metal tube. Wait, that wasn't a shadow! It's something moving... Solid metal... Kind of shieldlike affair rising up out of the cylinder... It's going higher and higher. Why, it's standing on legs... Actually rearing up on a sort of metal framework. Now it's reaching above the trees and the searchlights are on it. Hold on!'

The announcer is back with a grave announcement. Incredible as it may seem, he says, those strange beings who landed in the Jersey farmlands are the vanguard of an invading army from the planet Mars. The battle that took place at Grover's Mill has ended in one of the most startling defeats ever suffered by any army in modern times; 7,000 men armed with rifles and machine guns pitted against a single fighting machine of the invaders from Mars. There are 120 known survivors. The rest are strewn over the battle area from Grover's Mill to Plainsboro, crushed and trampled to death under the metal feet of the monster, or burned to cinders by its Heat-Ray.

We hear that the monster is now in control of the middle section of New Jersey and has effectively cut the state through its centre. Communication lines are down from Pennsylvania to the Atlantic Ocean. Railroad tracks have been torn up and highways to the north, south and west are clogged with frantic human traffic. Police and army reserves cannot control the mad flight and by morning the fugitives will have swelled Philadelphia, Camden and Trenton to twice their normal population. Martial law prevails throughout New Jersey and eastern Pennsylvania.

It is announced that the Secretary of the Interior will now speak to the nation from Washington. The role is played by Kenny Delmar, sounding uncannily like President Franklin D. Roosevelt. The Secretary of the Interior tells America that he will not attempt to conceal the gravity of the situation that confronts the country, nor the government's concern in protecting the lives and property of its people. But he wishes to impress upon all private citizens and public officials the urgent need for calm and resourceful action. He says that 'this formidable enemy' is confined to a comparatively small area 'and we may place our faith in the military forces to keep them there. In the meantime placing our faith in God we must continue the performance of our duties each and every one of us, so that we may confront this destructive adversary with a nation united, courageous and consecrated to the preservation of human supremacy on this earth. I thank you.'

\* \* \*

It was during this part of the broadcast that the control room telephone rang and Davidson Taylor was summoned out of the studio. Houseman remembers that he quickly returned 'pale as death' and told the rest of the team that they must interrupt the show on orders from CBS top brass. He was reminded that a station break was scheduled to come up shortly, so there was no need for anyone to enter the studio and disturb the actors' concentration. Taylor told Houseman that 'a kind of madness' had erupted around the broadcast and the network's switchboards had become 'swamped into uselessness'. He said that rumours were coming in of deaths, suicides and panic injuries.

\* \* \*

The announcer is back with 'bulletins too numerous to read piling up in the studio here'. He says that the central portion of New Jersey is blacked out from radio communication due to the effect of the Heat-Ray upon power lines and electrical equipment. Cables offering assistance have been received from English, French and German scientific bodies. Astronomers report seeing continued gas outbursts at regular intervals on Mars. Attempts have been made to locate Professor Pierson of Princeton, who observed the aliens at close range. It is feared he was lost in the recent battle. Reports from Langham Field, Virginia, say that surveillance planes report three Martian machines visible above treetops, moving north towards Somerville with local people fleeing ahead of them. Although Heat-Rays are not in use, the Martians are advancing at express-train speed. The invaders only stop to uproot power lines, bridges and railroad tracks. Their apparent objective is to crush resistance, paralyse communication, and disorganise human society.

A bulletin from Basking Ridge, New Jersey, says that coon hunters have stumbled on a second cylinder, similar to the first, embedded in the great swamp twenty miles south of Morristown. The army is proceeding from Newark to blow up the second invading unit before the cylinder opens and the fighting machine is rigged. They are taking up positions in the foothills of the Watchung Mountains. Another bulletin from Langham Field reports that scouting planes have spotted three enemy machines increasing speed northwards, kicking over houses and trees in their evident haste to form a conjunction with their allies south of Morristown. Machines have also been sighted by a telephone operator within ten miles of Plainfield. A bulletin from Winston Field, Long Island, claims that a fleet of army bombers carrying heavy explosives is flying north in pursuit of the alien enemies. Surveillance planes are acting as guides, keeping the speeding enemy in sight.

'Just a moment please,' says the announcer urgently. 'Ladies and gentlemen, we've run special wires to the artillery line in adjacent villages to give you direct reports in the zone of the advancing enemy. First we take you to the battery of the 22nd Field Artillery, located in the Watchtung Mountains.'

An artillery officer (Richard Wilson) is heard plotting the range of a field gun with a gunner (William Alland). Heavy gunfire is heard. A field artillery observer (Stefan Schnabel) claims that one of the invaders has been hit. Black smoke appears to be heading in the direction of the field artillery. The smoke turns out to be poisonous gas. The artillerymen don their gas masks. There is coughing and wheezing as they fall to the ground.

There is a pause, followed by the sound of aircraft engines. In the cockpit of a military aircraft is Bomber Lieutenant Voght (Howard Smith) telling his base over the radio that he is in command of eight army V-8-43 bombers, off Bayonne, New Jersey. He reports that enemy tripod machines are in sight, reinforced by three machines from the Morristown cylinder, making six altogether. One machine is crippled – believed to have been hit by a shell from an army gun in the Watchung Mountains. A heavy and dense black fog hangs close to the earth, nature unknown. There is no sign of a Heat-Ray. The enemy turns east, crossing the Passaic River into the Jersey marshes. Another straddles the Pulaski Skyway. Their objective is New York City. They are pushing down a high-tension power station. The machines are close together and bombers ready to attack. Planes are circling, ready to strike. Just 1,000 yards to go... 800 yards... 600... 400... 200... There they go! A giant arm is raised from one of the enemy machines. The sound of a Heat-Ray. There is a green flash. 'They're spraying us with flame,' cries Bomber Voght. 'Engines are giving out at 2,000 feet. No chance to release bombs. Only one thing left... Drop on them, plane and all. We're diving on the first one. Now the engine's gone...'

There is the sound of a plane crashing, followed by a pause and then the voices of radio operators (Frank Readick and William Herz) talking to each other.

OPERATOR ONE: This is Bayonne, New Jersey, calling Langham Field... This is Bayonne, New Jersey, calling Langham Field... Come in, please...

OPERATOR TWO: This is Langham Field... Go ahead...

OPERATOR ONE: Eight army bombers in engagement with enemy tripod machines over Jersey flats. Engines incapacitated by Heat-Ray. All crashed. One enemy machine destroyed. Enemy now discharging heavy black smoke in direction of...

OPERATOR THREE: This is Newark, New Jersey... This is Newark, New Jersey... Warning! Poisonous black smoke pouring in from Jersey marshes. Reaches South Street. Gas masks useless. Urge population to move into open spaces... Automobiles use Routes 7, 23, 24... Avoid congested areas. Smoke now spreading over Raymond Boulevard...

OPERATOR FOUR: 2X2L... Calling CQ.... 2X2L... Calling CQ... 2X2L... Calling 8X3R... Come in, please...

OPERATOR FIVE: This is 8X3R... coming back at 2X2L.

OPERATOR FOUR: How's reception? How's reception? K, please. [A pause.] Where are you, 8X3R? What's the matter? Where are you?

Bells are heard ringing over New York City. A reporter (Ray Collins) positioned on the rooftop of the Broadcasting Building informs listeners that bells are warning people to evacuate the city as Martians approach. In the last two hours, at least 3 million people have moved out along the roads to the north. Hutchinson River Parkway is still open for motor traffic. The public should avoid bridges to Long Island as they are jammed. All communication with Jersey shore was closed ten minutes ago. 'There are no more defences, our army is wiped out... Artillery, air force, everything wiped out. This may be the last broadcast. We'll stay here to the end... People are holding services below us... in the cathedral. [Voices singing hymns can be heard.] Now I look down the harbour. All manner of boats, overloaded with fleeing population, are pulling out from the docks. [Sound of boat whistles.] Streets are all jammed. Noise in crowds like New Year's Eve in the city.'

Hurriedly he continues, 'Wait a minute... Enemy now in sight above the Palisades. Five great machines. First one is crossing river. I can see it from here, wading the Hudson like a man wading through a brook... A bulletin's handed me... Martian cylinders are falling all over the country. One outside Buffalo, one in Chicago, St Louis... Seem to be timed and spaced. Now the first machine reaches the shore. He stands watching, looking over the city. His steel, cowlish head is even with the skyscrapers. He waits for the others. They rise like a line of new towers on the city's west side... Now they're lifting their metal hands. This is the end now. Smoke comes out... Black smoke, drifting over the city. People in the streets see it now. They're running towards the East River... Thousands of them, dropping in like rats. Now the smoke's spreading faster. It's reached Times Square. People trying to run away from it, but it's no use. They're falling like flies. Now the smoke's crossing Sixth Avenue... Fifth Avenue... 100 yards away... It's 50 feet...'

There is the sound of a body collapsing onto the ground.

A radio operator repeats, 'This is 2X2L calling CQ... 2X2L calling CQ... 2X2L calling CQ... New York. Isn't there anyone on the air? Isn't there anyone on the air? Isn't there anyone...? 2X2L...'

There is five seconds of total silence – 'dead air time' as it is known in broadcasting circles – followed by the suave and bright tones of announcer Dan Seymour, back on the air forty minutes and twenty-six seconds after the programme first began. He reminds listeners that they are tuned into a CBS presentation of Orson Welles and *The Mercury Theatre on the Air* in an original dramatisation of *The War of the Worlds* by H. G. Wells. He says that the performance will continue after a brief intermission.

Following a musical interlude, we are reunited with Professor Pierson, who is in hiding in an empty house in Grover's Mill, writing his notes, obsessed by the thought that he may be the last living man on earth. He looks at his blackened hands, torn shoes and tattered clothes and tries to connect them with the professor who lived at Princeton, and who on the night of 30 October glimpsed through his telescope an orange splash of light on a distant planet. The morning sun streams in through a window. The black cloud of gas has lifted and the scorched meadows to the north look like a black snowstorm has passed across them. He ventures outside the house and heads towards a road. There is no traffic but here and there a wrecked car, overturned baggage or a blackened skeleton can be seen. He pushes on north, feeling safer trailing the alien monsters instead of running away from them. He walks in a northerly direction for two days through a desolate world. Finally he notices a living creature... a small red squirrel in a beech tree. He stares at the animal and the animal stares back, and Pierson believes at that moment that he and the squirrel share the same emotion – the joy of finding another living being.

The next day he reaches Newark – undemolished, but humbled by some whim of the advancing Martians. With an odd feeling of being watched, he catches sight of something crouching in a doorway. He moves towards it, and it rises up and becomes a man – a man wearing a uniform and armed with a large knife.

The stranger (Carl Frank) demands to know where Pierson has come from. He tells him he is from Princeton. 'Is that near Grover's Mill?' he is asked. Pierson says that it is and the stranger angrily informs him that there is no food to be found in this place. This is his country and there is only food for one. 'So, which way are you going?'

They move into a doorway to talk. The stranger says that the aliens have headed off towards New York. He says that during the day they are not seen, but at night the sky is alive with their lights. Days before, he witnessed two of them dragging something large across the flats near the airport. 'I believe they're learning how to fly,' he tells Pierson.

The stranger says that the invaders 'wrecked the greatest country in the world… There isn't anything to do. We're done. We're licked.' He tells Pierson that he was a member of the National Guard, which is why he is wearing a uniform. He predicts that the Martians will soon begin catching survivors, keeping the best and storing them in cages. They haven't begun yet, he says. He says that instead of rushing around blind, any survivors need to fix themselves up according to the way things are now and not how they used to be with cities, nations, civilization, progress – which is now all finished.

'If that's so, what is there left to live for?' asks Pierson. The stranger replies that there won't be any more concerts for a million years or so, and no nice little dinners at restaurants. If it's amusement you're after, I guess the game's up.

The stranger tells Pierson that he wants to live and not be exterminated. He says he doesn't plan to be caught and tamed, fattened or bred like an ox either. He plans to go right in, under the invader's feet, and live free while learning how to survive. It isn't all of us that were made for wild beasts, he says. 'And that's what it's got to be… All these little office workers that used to live in these houses, they'd be no good. They haven't any stuff to 'em. They just used to run off to work. I've seen hundreds of 'em, running wild to catch their commuter train in the morning for fear they'd get canned if they didn't; running back at night afraid they won't be in time for dinner. Lives insured and a little invested in case of accidents. And on Sundays, worried about the hereafter. The Martians will be a godsend for those guys. Nice roomy cages, good food, careful breeding, no worries. After a week or so chasing about the fields on empty stomachs, they'll come and be glad to be caught.'

Pierson says the man has it all figured out.

'You bet I have,' says the stranger, 'and that isn't all. These Martians will make pets of some of 'em, train 'em to do tricks. Who knows? Get sentimental over the pet boy who grew up and had to be killed. And some, maybe, they'll train to hunt us.'

The stranger says that survivors will live underground, in the sewers. 'Under New York are miles and miles of 'em. The main ones are big enough for anybody. Then there's cellars, vaults, underground storerooms, railway tunnels, subways… And we'll get a bunch of strong men together. No weak ones; that rubbish… out.'

Pierson hears how survivors will have to find safe places to live. They will get all the books they can, especially science books. 'That's where men like you come in, see?' he tells Pierson. 'We'll raid the museums; we'll even spy on the Martians. It may not be so much we have to learn before… Imagine this: four or five of their own fighting machines suddenly start off… Heat-Rays right and left and not a Martian in 'em. But men, who have learned the way how. It may even be in our time. Gee! Imagine having one of them lovely things with its Heat-Ray wide and free! We'd turn it on Martians, we'd turn it on men. We'd bring everybody down to their knees.'

'Is that your plan?' asks Pierson.

'Yes,' says the stranger, 'You and me and a few more of us, we'd own the world.'

Pierson gets up to leave.

'Say, what's the matter? Where are you going?' the stranger calls to Pierson.

'Not to your world,' Pierson answers. 'Goodbye, stranger.'

After parting with the stranger, Pierson arrives at the Holland Tunnel, anxious to know the fate of the great city on the other side of the Hudson. Cautiously he emerges and makes his way up Canal Street. He reaches 14th Street, where black powder covers the ground. Several bodies are found and an evil smell is emitting from the gratings of cellars below some houses.

He wanders through the city and stands alone on Times Square. He catches sight of a lean dog running down 7th Avenue with a piece of dark brown meat in his jaws, a pack of starving mongrels at its heels. He walks up Broadway, past silent shop windows displaying their mute wares to empty sidewalks. Near Columbus Circle he notices models of 1939 motorcars in a showroom facing empty streets. From over the top of the General Motors Building, he watches a flock of black birds circling in the sky.

Suddenly he catches sight of the hood of a Martian machine, standing somewhere in Central Park, gleaming in the afternoon sun. He rushes into the park, where standing in a silent row along the mall are nineteen great metal Titans, their cowls empty, their great steel arms hanging listlessly by their sides.

Pierson looks in vain for the monsters that once inhabited the machines. His eyes are attracted to a flock of black birds hovering directly above. They circle to the ground and there before his eyes, stark and silent, lay the Martians, with the hungry birds pecking and tearing brown shreds of flesh from their dead bodies. Later, when their bodies are examined in laboratories, it is discovered that they were killed by the 'putrefactive and disease bacteria against which their systems were unprepared, slain by the humblest things that God, in his wisdom, has put upon the Earth'.

* * *

For the last few moments Welles had been alone at the microphone, totally immersed in the role of Professor Pierson. The rest of the cast had no further lines and had stood away from their own microphones. They noticed that the control room on the other side of the soundproof glass was starting to fill up with people – including a number of bewildered-looking policemen.

As the closing music swelled up, Welles continued speaking into the microphone, as himself. By then, he too had noticed the crowd in the control booth. In 1955 he told the BBC, 'There were a great many policemen, and every moment, more. Later we found out that the police were as confused as we were, because there wasn't anything they could arrest us for. But there they were, looking fierce; a lot of people talking to other people in a dumb show and a very tense atmosphere was generated in the studio. We thought that something had gone wrong; some few people had complained and have swallowed what we had told them about the Martians coming to Earth. But we didn't know that it wasn't a few people, it was in fact nationwide. I had no idea that I'd suddenly become a sort of… national event!'

Lightening the tone of his voice, with an eye on his script and the other on the crowd behind the soundproof glass, he brought the programme to a close:

> This is Orson Welles, ladies and gentlemen, out of character to assure you that *The War of the Worlds* has no further significance than as the holiday offering it was intended to be. The Mercury Theatre's own radio version of dressing up in a sheet and jumping out of a bush and saying, 'Boo!' Starting now, we couldn't soap all your windows and steal all your garden gates by tomorrow night… So we did the best next thing. We annihilated the world before your very ears, and utterly destroyed the CBS. You will be relieved, I hope, to learn that we didn't mean it, and that both institutions are still open for business. So goodbye everybody, and remember the terrible lesson you learned tonight. That grinning, glowing, globular invader of your living room is an inhabitant of the pumpkin patch, and if your doorbell rings and nobody's there, that was no Martian… It's Halloween!'

Bernard Herrmann conducted the Mercury theme while Dan Seymour closed the programme: 'Tonight the Columbia Broadcasting System and its affiliated stations coast-to-coast have brought you *The War of the Worlds,* by H. G. Wells, the seventeenth in its weekly series of dramatic broadcasts featuring Orson Welles and *The Mercury Theatre on the Air*. Next week we present a dramatisation of three famous short stories. This is the Columbia Broadcasting System.'

A studio engineer addressed the actors through a speaker from the other side of the soundproof glass. 'Thank you everybody. I suggest you all stay where you are for the moment. There appears to be a bit of a problem somewhere.'

CHAPTER EIGHT

# Of Course,
# I'm Terribly Sorry Now

*'This only goes to show, my beamish boy, that the intelligent people were all listening to a dummy and all the dummies were listening to you.'*
*—Telegram to Orson Welles from his friend Alexander Woollcott, American critic and commentator, 31 October 1938*

Welles was anxious to get out of the studio and back to his *Danton's Death* dress rehearsal at the Mercury Theatre, where impatient actors were waiting to continue where they had left off eight hours previously. The police, however, had other ideas.

According to Houseman, the first calls from frightened radio listeners arrived shortly after the Martians had landed at Grover's Mill. Although unaware of what was going on outside the cocooned radio studio, he later learned that all hell had broken loose on the CBS switchboards several floors below as the public called in demanding to know what was going on. Later, as the studio began to fill with an assortment of policemen and worried CBS executives, Houseman 'suddenly realised that the spoken word, through radio, was able to affect the feelings and emotions of the entire world'.

William Herz, a cast member, recalled, 'This was the only time that, in all the years that I worked with Orson, I ever saw him slightly afraid. I don't think that he quite knew what was going to happen. It's very possible that he thought that this could have ended his career – but it did exactly the opposite.'

Harold 'Hal' Davis, a twenty-two-year-old CBS publicity manager, remembered, 'About ten or fifteen minutes into the programme the 'phones started ringing and we began getting hysterical calls from people claiming that the Martians had landed and asking what they should do. I told them, "Come on – this is just Orson Welles and the Mercury Theatre." I had the programme on as well and was listening to it through the monitor, so I told everyone to take it easy, as it was just a Sunday night play. Don't panic, I said. There are no invaders.'

All the same, Davis thought it best to telephone the control room to tell someone about the commotion going on in American radioland. Said Davis,

'I asked them to tell Orson Welles that people were taking the programme seriously and they had better put out a disclaimer. But the studio refused to interrupt the actors or the programme and simply carried on. A little while later the chief telephone operator came back on the line to me and said, "Hal, it's gotten away from me and I can't handle it."'

There is confusion over what William S. Paley, founder and president of CBS, was up to that night. William Alland claims that from his place behind a microphone he saw a worried-looking Paley through the soundproofed glass enter the studio with other network bosses 'wearing pajamas, bedroom slippers and a bathrobe'. Paley himself recalled that he was at home in his palatial Long Island residence, not listening to the radio but 'playing cards'. He remembered, 'These telephone calls were coming in and they wouldn't say what they wanted, but demanded to speak to me. And I thought these people were calling in to make some complaints. I was getting these kinds of calls all the time. One of the callers said they were from my office, so I spoke to them and they said that this terrible thing had happened and it sounded as if the whole country had burst wide open.'

Paley was not wrong. Once the play came off air, Davidson Taylor was the first to open the door linking the control room to the studio. All the actors were instructed to go through to a small office along the corridor, and each was told to hand in his script to someone at the other side waiting to collect them. Welles, Houseman and Herrmann were escorted to a back office 'for questioning'. As they passed through the control room someone yelled that there was a telephone call for Welles. Houseman remembered, 'A shrill voice through the receiver announced itself as belonging to the mayor of some Midwestern city, one of the big ones. He was screaming at Welles. Choking with fury, he reported mobs in the streets of his city, women and children huddled in churches, violence and looting. If, as he has just learned, the whole thing was nothing but a crummy joke, then he, personally, said he was coming to New York to punch the author of it on the nose!' Welles quickly hung up.

Down on the ground-floor lobby of the CBS Building, police were holding back an army of reporters and photographers sent to cover the story, with orders to get interviews with Welles or any of his actors. At the same time, police officers were attempting to stop frightened members of the public from getting into the building and cast and musicians from getting out. Some actors had managed to slip through the police net on the twenty-second floor and were ordered back up in the elevator 'for questioning about your part in this incident'.

Several CBS musicians, afraid they might miss their last train home, went up in the elevator for a few floors before getting out and escaping from the building via some unguarded back stairs.

Houseman described the following hours as 'a nightmare'. He added, 'We are hurried out of the studio, downstairs, into a back office. Here we sit incommunicado while network employees are busily collecting, destroying or locking up all scripts and records of the broadcast. Then the press is let loose upon us, ravening for horror. How many deaths have *we* heard of (implying that they have heard of thousands)? What do *we* know of the fatal stampede in a Jersey hall (implying that it is one of many)? What traffic deaths (the ditches must be chocked with corpses)? The suicides (haven't you heard about the one on Riverside Drive)? It is all quite vague in my memory and quite terrible.'

Instead of placing Welles, Houseman and Herrmann under studio house arrest, the police allowed the men to sneak out through a back exit. Welles and Houseman scurried down to their theatre like hunted animals to their hole to find actors stoically rehearsing – and more press lying in wait. Welles climbed onto the stage to explain to his cast what had happened, but the photographers caught him with his eyes raised up to heaven and arms extended in an attitude of crucifixion. And for a short time afterwards, it looked as if the entire company working for *The Mercury Theatre on the Air* had been nailed onto the same cross.

Looking like an early Christian saint about to be thrown to the lions, Welles addressed the actors at the Mercury Theatre after the police allowed him to leave the radio studio. (*Library of Congress*)

Meanwhile, CBS agreed to make a series of on-air announcements to people still listening to the radio as the night progressed. Hal Davis typed out the hurried statement:

> For those listeners who tuned into Orson Welles' *Mercury Theatre on the Air* broadcast from 8 to 9 p.m. tonight and did not realise that the programme was merely a modernised adaptation of H. G. Wells' famous novel *The War of the Worlds*, we are repeating the fact which was made clear four times on the programme, that while the names of some American cities were used, as in all novels and dramatizations, the entire story and all of its incidents were fictitious.

Columnist and broadcaster Walter Winchell, whose Sunday evening programme went out on a rival network half an hour after *The Mercury Theatre on the Air* had finished, told his listeners: 'Mr And Mrs America, there is no cause for alarm! America has not fallen. I repeat, America has not fallen!'

\* \* \*

It had been a quiet Sunday in Port Norris, a sleepy little town between Atlantic City and Philadelphia, until sometime around 8.30 p.m. The telephone began to ring incessantly at the local police station and officer 'V. M.' noticed that the traffic heading down Main Street had suddenly gone wild.

Hundreds of cars began to flash along at speeds that normally indicated robbers were rushing away from the scene of a bank raid. But there were family parties in most of the cars; the women and children could not all be gun molls and child racketeers. When a motorcycle cop attempted to overtake one speeding auto, two or three others passed him. The stampede was in all directions and everyone was heading for the hills. Nobody would stop for a policeman's hail. Now and then, a traffic man would catch an incoherent shout that there was an 'invasion' and that 'the world was coming to an end'.

Later that evening, 'V. M.' reached for his fountain pen and wrote up his log for 30 October:

> Between 8.30–10.00 p.m. received numerous phone calls as a result of WABC broadcast this evening re: Mars attacking this country. Calls included papers, police departments including NYC [New York City] and private persons. No record kept of some due to working Teletype and all three extensions ringing at same time. At least 50 calls were answered. Persons calling inquiring as to meteors, number of persons killed, gas attack, militia being called out and fires. All were advised nothing unusual had occurred and that rumours were due to a radio dramatization of a play.

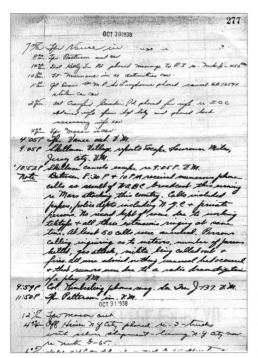

A log produced on 30 October 1938 by the New Jersey State Police's duty officer at Port Norris. (*John Gosling, www.war-of-the-worlds.co.uk*)

The initial puzzlement was not restricted to officer 'V. M.'. Policemen across the whole of America were also receiving telephone demands for gas masks and information as to the safest place to hide from alien invaders. Priests and clergymen were startled by the rush of requests for instant confessions and astonished by the number of interruptions to sermons from people pleading for prayers to be said to avert the impending end of the world. Hospital staff were also puzzled by the number of nervous wrecks and falling-downstairs cases calling for their attention that night.

The frightened population was slow to discover the cause of the national panic because the panic-stricken had different stories to tell. They had tuned in at different periods during the CBS broadcast and all had different ideas about the 'invasion'. Some said there were octopus-like Martian monsters armed with poison gas and Heat-Rays, while others cried that Armageddon was on its way. Many identified the invaders as Germans, others as Japanese.

It was hours before the panic died down, thanks to the NYPD, which sent out the following message: 'To all receivers: Station WABC informs us that the recent broadcast over that station was a dramatisation of a play. No cause for alarm.'

The New Jersey State Police teletyped a 'note to all receivers – WABC broadcast as drama re this section being attacked by residents of Mars. Imaginary affair.'

The Associated Press wired a statement to newspapers and radio stations across the country: 'Note to Editors: Queries to newspapers from radio listeners throughout the United States tonight regarding a reported meteor fall which killed a number of New Jerseyites are the result of a studio dramatisation of a play. No cause for alarm.'

But the media chose to ignore this advice. The Martian panic broadcast was a great story, too good to kill and good enough to keep running for two or three days. And while reporters were sent forth to obtain 'quotes' from 'nervous Americans,' sub-editors sharpened their pencils before jotting down sensational headlines for the following morning's front pages.

\* \* \*

The next morning, the 'Martian invasion' was headline news everywhere across the United States from New York to Los Angeles, Okmulgee to Thief River Falls, Hicksville to Hackensack. Every newspaper was appalled that a radio play should disguise itself as a news programme, fooling people into thinking that aliens from space had really invaded – and conquered – their 'sweet land of liberty'. The papers were shocked, outraged, incredulous and hysterical. They thundered, they roared and they demanded explanations. Copy read 'mass hysteria', 'panic spread across the nation', 'terror spread by hoax', 'many flee homes to escape', 'prayers for deliverance' and 'Washington may act'. They looked for someone to blame – and the name on everyone's lips was Orson Welles.

Hal Davis and his CBS publicity team did their best to explain the situation and laboured long after the broadcast to make clear what had happened and why.

There were rumbles from across the Atlantic, too, where H. G. Wells himself hinted at legal trouble for CBS if a 'retraction' was not forthcoming. His US agent, Jacques Chambrun, said:

> In the name of H. G. Wells I granted CBS the right to dramatise his novel *The War of the Worlds* for one performance over the radio. It was not explained to me that this dramatisation would be made with a liberty that amounts to a complete rewriting of the novel and renders it into an entirely different story.
>
> Mr Wells and I consider that by doing so CBS and Mr Orson Welles have far overstepped their rights in the matter and believe that CBS should make a full retraction. Mr H. G. Wells personally is deeply concerned that any work of his should be used in such a way, and with totally unwarranted liberty, to cause deep distress and alarm throughout the United States.

A hastily arranged press conference was called by CBS at its New York studio on the afternoon of Monday 31 October – Halloween Day – and

*The War of the Worlds* 'panic broadcast' was front-page news in papers and cinema newsreels across America on the day after its historic broadcast in October 1938. (*Author's collection; Critical Past*)

Welles is surrounded by reporters and cameramen at a hastily arranged press conference at CBS studios, where he expressed 'my deep regret over any misapprehension that our broadcast might have created among some listeners'. (*Author's collection*)

the network ordered Welles to attend. The man who had scared the nation arrived alone, eyes red from lack of sleep and with three days worth of beard on his face. He wanted to be anywhere else but sharing a room with reporters, photographers and newsreel cameramen. As soon as he entered the meeting room, a barrage of questions was fired in his direction. He sat in the centre of the press corps, looking like a lamb before slaughter, and read from a prepared statement scribbled that morning and sent to CBS for approval:

Despite my deep regret over any misapprehension that our broadcast might have created among some listeners, I am even more bewildered over this misunderstanding in the light of an analysis of the broadcast itself. It seems to me that there are four factors which should have in any event maintained the illusion of fiction in the broadcast. The first was that the broadcast was performed as if occurring in the future, and as if it were then related by a survivor of a past occurrence. The date of this fanciful invasion of this planet by Martians was clearly given as 1939 and was so announced at the outset of the broadcast.

The second element was the fact that the broadcast took place at our weekly Mercury Theatre period and had been so announced in all the papers. For seventeen consecutive weeks we have been broadcasting radio shows. Sixteen of these seventeen broadcasts have been fiction and have been presented as such. Only one in the series was a true story, the broadcast of *Hell on Ice* by Commander Ellsberg and was identified as a true story in the framework of radio drama.

The third element was the fact that at the very outset of the broadcast, and twice during its enactment, listeners were told that this was a play, an adaptation of an old novel by H. G. Wells. Furthermore, at the conclusion, a detailed statement to this effect was made.

The fourth factor seems to me to have been the most pertinent of all. That is the familiarity of the fable, within the American idiom, of Mars and the Martians. For many decades 'the Man from Mars' has been almost a synonym for fantasy. In very old morgues of many newspapers there will be found a series of grotesque cartoons that ran daily, which gave this fantasy imaginary form. As a matter of fact, the fantasy as such has been used in radio programmes many times. In these broadcasts, conflict between citizens of Mars and other planets has been a familiarly accepted fairy-tale. The same make-believe is familiar to newspaper readers through a comic strip that uses the same device.

Far from expecting the radio audience to take the programme as fact rather than as a fictional presentation, we feared that the classic H. G. Wells story, which has served as inspiration for so many moving pictures, radio serials and even comic strips, might appear too old fashioned for modern consumption. We can only suppose that the special nature of radio, which is often heard in fragments, or in parts disconnected from the whole, has led to this misunderstanding.

Looking at his watch and itching to get out of the building and back to the *Danton's Death* rehearsals, Welles was then grilled by the news-hungry reporters:

Q: Were you aware of the terror such a broadcast would stir up?

WELLES: Definitely not. You must realise that when I left the broadcast last night I went into a dress rehearsal for a play that's opening in two days – *Danton's Death* – and I've had almost no sleep. So I know less about this than you do. I haven't read the papers. I'm terribly shocked by the effect it's had. The technique I used was not original with me, or peculiar to the Mercury Theatre's presentation. It was not even new. I anticipated nothing unusual.

Q: Would you do the show over again?

WELLES: I won't say I won't follow this technique again, as it is a legitimate dramatic form.

Q: Do you think there ought to be a law against such enactments as we had last night?

WELLES: I don't know what the legislation would be. I know that almost everyone in radio would do almost everything to avert the kind of thing that happened last night, myself included. Radio is new and we are still learning about the effect it has on people.

Q: When were you first aware of the trouble caused?

WELLES: Immediately after the broadcast was finished, when people told me of the large number of 'phone calls received.

Q: Should you have toned down the language of the drama?

WELLES: No. You don't play murder in soft words.

Q: Why was the story changed to put in the names of American cities and government officers?

WELLES: H. G. Wells used real cities in Europe, and to make the play more acceptable to American listeners, we used real cities in America. Of course, I'm terribly sorry now.

Before departing, Welles commented that the Mercury Theatre had received 'numerous telegrams from listeners saying how much they liked the show'.

* * *

Howard Koch was not needed at the studio for rehearsals or the live broadcast and remained at home to listen to his play. Afterwards he went to bed and slept like a log, blissfully unaware of what was happening outside. At about midnight Houseman called to break the news but Koch was too exhausted to hear the telephone ringing.

The following morning was traditionally Koch's day off and he gave himself the luxury of a late lie-in. At around lunchtime he went out to get a haircut, noticing that people in the street were huddled together, deep in conversation.

As he passed one group he heard the worlds 'invasion' and 'panic' mentioned and jumped to the conclusion that Hitler had invaded some new territory and that the war all Americans dreaded had finally broken out.

When Koch questioned his barber what was going on, the hairdresser broke out into a broad grin and held up the front page of a newspaper with the headline 'Nation in Panic from Martian Broadcast'.

Koch remembered, 'This was a moment that still seems unreal to me. I stared at the paper while the confused barber stared at me. Centre page was a picture of Orson, his arms outstretched in a gesture of helpless innocence, and underneath was the opening scenes of my play.'

Although unaware of it at the time, something was sitting on Koch's coffee table back at his apartment that would later become very valuable – a copy of the forty-seven-page *The War of the Worlds* script, one of only two known to have survived. Nobody ever asked him to turn his copy over alongside others handed in by the cast and technicians. So he hung on to it for the next fifty years.

CHAPTER NINE

# Don't Panic!

*'The fate of a nation was riding that night.'*
*—Henry Wadsworth Longfellow*

Tens of thousands of words were hammered out on the typewriters of news reporters across America on the night of Sunday 30 October. Bearing in mind that the 'Martian invasion' story did not begin to break until after 8 p.m., it is amazing how reporters working on the East Coast managed to gather so much information before first editions of their newspapers went to press.

The reporters must have been thankful that the Mercury Theatre's panic broadcast was transmitted on a Sunday, a traditionally 'slow day' for news, meaning that the print media had plenty of stories that could instantly be 'pulled' to make way for late news sent in by staff reporters and wire services.

Most newspapers, more or less, carried similar stories about how people living in their own circulation areas reacted to the broadcast. Perhaps the best account appeared in *The New York Times*, a paper with an early deadline for its first edition, but which still managed to get the entire story out in time to hit the streets at 6 a.m. the following morning. The story ran:

RADIO LISTENERS IN PANIC, TAKING WAR DRAMA AS FACT

*Many Flee Homes to Escape 'Gas Raid From Mars' – Phone Calls Swamp Police at Broadcast of Wells Fantasy*

A wave of mass hysteria seized thousands of radio listeners between 8.15 and 9.30 o'clock last night when a broadcast of a dramatization of H. G. Wells' fantasy, *The War of the Worlds*, led thousands to believe that an interplanetary conflict had started with invading Martians spreading wide death and destruction in New Jersey and New York.

The broadcast, which disrupted households, interrupted religious services, created traffic jams and clogged communications systems, was made by

# The New York Times

Copyright. 1938, by The New York Times Company.

Second-Class Matter.
New York, N. Y.

NEW YORK, MONDAY, OCTOBER 31, 1938.

P P

## MEAD STANDS PAT AS A NEW DEALER IN BID FOR SENATE

### Democratic Candidate Opposes Any Except Minor Changes in Labor and Security Laws

### UPHOLDS THEORY OF TVA

### Wants Budget Balanced, but Not if This Means 'Misery,' He Tells The Times

*Text of Representative Mead's reply is printed on Page 6.*

**From a Staff Correspondent**

BUFFALO, N. Y., Oct. 30.—Representatives James M. Mead, Democratic candidate for the short-term Senatorial seat in the election Nov. 8, today answered in a statement the six questions on campaign issues propounded by THE NEW YORK TIMES to the four New York nominees of the two major parties in an editorial Oct. 20.

Mr. Mead's answer, in the main, was a broad and little qualified defense of the New Deal legislation which he, as a member of the House of Representatives, had a part in formulating and passing.

The principles of the Social Security and National Labor Relations Acts he defended stoutly, seeing need only for revisions to extend the benefits of the former, a correction of technical defects and a tightening of administration.

Principal opposition to the Social Security Act he saw inspired by those who fear that it will "become too important a monument to the Democratic party and to men like President Roosevelt and Senator Wagner."

**Opposes "Pay-as-You-Go" Policy**

He unqualifiedly opposed a revision of the law to make social se-

## Radio Listeners in Panic, Taking War Drama as Fact

### Many Flee Homes to Escape 'Gas Raid From Mars'—Phone Calls Swamp Police at Broadcast of Wells Fantasy

A wave of mass hysteria seized thousands of radio listeners throughout the nation between 8:15 and 9:30 o'clock last night when a broadcast of a dramatization of H. G. Wells's fantasy, "The War of the Worlds," led thousands to believe that an interplanetary conflict had started with invading Martians spreading wide death and destruction in New Jersey and New York.

The broadcast, which disrupted households, interrupted religious services, created traffic jams and clogged communications systems, was made by Orson Welles, who as the radio character, "The Shadow," used to give "the creeps" to countless child listeners. This time at least a score of adults required medical treatment for shock and hysteria.

In Newark, in a single block at Heddon Terrace and Hawthorne Avenue, more than twenty families rushed out of their houses with wet handkerchiefs and towels over their faces to flee from what they believed was to be a gas raid. Some began moving household furniture.

Throughout New York families left their homes, some to flee to near-by parks. Thousands of persons called the police, newspapers

and radio stations here and in other cities of the United States and Canada seeking advice on protective measures against the raids.

The program was produced by Mr. Welles and the Mercury Theatre on the Air over station WABC and the Columbia Broadcasting System's coast-to-coast network from 8 to 9 o'clock.

The radio play, as presented, was to simulate a regular radio program with a "break-in" for the material of the play. The radio listeners, apparently, missed or did not listen to the introduction, which was: "The Columbia Broadcasting System and its affiliated stations present Orson Welles and the Mercury Theatre on the Air in 'The War of the Worlds' by H. G. Wells."

They also failed to associate the program with the newspaper listing of the program, announced as "Today: 8:00-9:00—Play: H. G. Wells's 'War of the Worlds'—WABC." They ignored three additional announcements made during the broadcast emphasizing its fictional nature.

Mr. Welles opened the program with a description of the series of

Continued on Page Four

## OUSTED JEWS FIN REFUGE IN POLAN AFTER BORDER ST

### Exiles Go to Relatives' Hor or to Camps Maintained Distribution Committee

### REVEAL CRUELTY OF TH

### Others Sent Back to Germa Pending Parleys on Issue the Two Governments

*Wireless to THE NEW YORK TIMES.*

WARSAW, Poland, Oct. 30.— evacuation from frontier area cording to official reports thousands of Polish Jews—8,000 12,000 according to an estimate the Jewish Relief Committee ported from Germany began to after they had been massed frontier stations up and down border for twenty-six hours. T terrible ordeal is nearing its en Polish authorities have permi officials of the Joint Distribu Committee to send the victim relatives' homes in Poland o special camps the committee m tains. The refugees spent a ni less night in barracks, crowded tion buildings or empty fre cars; many spent the night in open in the no man's land betw the frontiers.

The Joint Distribution Commi supplied food and will also pay cially reduced railway fares into interior.

It is believed that the evacua will last another day or so. M refugees desire to remain in frontier area pending the oute of the Warsaw-Berlin negotiati which may result in the repea the deportation order, enab them to return to their home Germany.

**Suffering Is Described**

Reports from various points a the frontier describe the terr

## B. C. VLADECK DIES; CITY COUNCILMAN

### American Labor Party Chief Here Was Manager of The Jewish Daily Forward

B. Charney Vladeck, American

## DALADIER PREPARES TO RULE SEVERELY

### Calls Cabinet Meeting to Talk Over Decrees to Promote Recovery in Industry

By P. J. PHILIP

The New York Times reported the reaction to the broadcast on the cover of its Monday 31 October 1938 edition.

Orson Welles, who as the radio character, 'the Shadow', used to give 'the creeps' to countless child listeners. This time at least a score of adults required medical treatment for shock and hysteria.

In Newark, in a single block at Heddon Terrace and Hawthorne Avenue, more than twenty families rushed out of their houses with wet handkerchiefs and towels over their faces to flee from what they believed was to be a gas raid. Some began moving household furniture.

Throughout New York families left their homes, some to flee to near-by parks. Thousands of persons called the police, newspapers and radio stations here and in other cities of the United States and Canada seeking advice on protective measures against the raids.

The programme was produced by Mr Welles and *The Mercury Theatre on the Air* over station WABC and the Columbia Broadcasting System's coast-to-coast network, from 8 to 9 o'clock.

The radio play, as presented, was to simulate a regular radio program with a 'break-in' for the material of the play. The radio listeners, apparently, missed or did not listen to the introduction, which was: 'The Columbia Broadcasting System and its affiliated stations present Orson Welles and *The Mercury Theatre on the Air* in *The War of the Worlds* by H. G. Wells.'

They also failed to associate the program with the newspaper listing of the programme, announced as 'Today: 8.00–9.00 – Play: H. G. Wells's *The War of the Worlds* – WABC.' They ignored three additional announcements made during the broadcast emphasizing its fictional nature.

Mr Welles opened the programme with a description of the series of which it is a part. The simulated programme began. A weather report was given, prosaically. An announcer remarked that the programme would be continued from a hotel, with dance music. For a few moments a dance programme was given in the usual manner. Then there was a 'break-in' with a 'flash' about a professor at an observatory noting a series of gas explosions on the planet Mars.

News bulletins and scene broadcasts followed, reporting, with the technique in which the radio had reported actual events, the landing of a 'meteor' near Princeton, NJ, 'killing' 1,500 persons, the discovery that the 'meteor' was a 'metal cylinder' containing strange creatures from Mars armed with 'death rays' to open hostilities against the inhabitants of the earth.

Despite the fantastic nature of the reported 'occurrences', the programme, coming after the recent war scare in Europe and a period in which the radio frequently had interrupted regularly scheduled programmes to report developments in the Czechoslovak situation, caused fright and panic throughout the area of the broadcast.

Telephone lines were tied up with calls from listeners or persons who had heard of the broadcasts. Many sought first to verify the reports. But large numbers, obviously in a state of terror, asked how they could follow the broadcast's advice and flee from the city, whether they would be safer in the 'gas raid' in the cellar or on the roof, how they could safeguard their children, and many of the questions which had been worrying residents of London and Paris during the tense days before the Munich agreement.

[...]

From one New York theatre a manager reported that a throng of playgoers had rushed from his theatre as a result of the broadcast. He said that the wives of two men in the audience, having heard the broadcast, called the theatre and insisted that their husbands be paged. This spread the 'news' to others in the audience.

The switchboard of *The New York Times* was overwhelmed by the calls. A total of 875 were received. One man who called from Dayton, Ohio, asked, 'What time will it be the end of the world?' A caller from the suburbs said he had had a houseful of guests and all had rushed out to the yard for safety.

Warren Dean, a member of the American Legion living in Manhattan who telephoned to verify the 'reports', expressed indignation which was typical of that of many callers.

'I've heard a lot of radio programmes, but I've never heard anything as rotten as that,' Mr Dean said. 'It was too realistic for comfort. They broke into a dance programme with a news flash. Everybody in my house was agitated by the news. It went on just like press radio news.'

At 9 o'clock a woman walked into the West 47th Street police station dragging two children, all carrying extra clothing. She said she was ready to leave the city. Police persuaded her to stay.

A garbled version of the reports reached the Dixie Bus Terminal, causing officials there to prepare to change their schedule on confirmation of 'news' of an accident at Princeton on their New Jersey route. Miss Dorothy Brown at the terminal sought verification, however, when the caller refused to talk with the dispatcher, explaining to her that 'the world is coming to an end and I have a lot to do'.

*Harlem Shaken by the 'News'*

Harlem was shaken by the 'news'. Thirty men and women rushed into the West 123rd Street police station and twelve into the West 135th Street station saying they had their household goods packed and were all ready to leave Harlem if the police would tell them where to go to be 'evacuated'. One man insisted he had heard 'the President's voice' over the radio, advising all citizens to leave the cities.

The parlor churches in the Negro district, congregations of the smaller sects meeting on the ground floors of brownstone houses, took the 'news' in stride as less faithful parishioners rushed in with it, seeking spiritual consolation. Evening services became 'end of the world' prayer meetings in some.

One man ran into the Wadsworth Avenue Police Station in Washington Heights, white with terror, crossing the Hudson River and asking what he should do. A man came in to the West 152nd Street Station, seeking traffic directions. The broadcast became a rumour that spread through the district and many persons stood on street corners hoping for a sight of the 'battle' in the skies.

In Queens the principal question asked of the switchboard operators at Police Headquarters was whether 'the wave of poison gas will reach as far as Queens'. Many said they were all packed up and ready to leave Queens when told to do so.

Samuel Tishman of 100 Riverside Drive was one of the multitude that fled into the street after hearing part of the programme. He declared that hundreds of persons evacuated their homes fearing that the 'city was being bombed'.

'I came home at 9.15 p.m. just in time to receive a telephone call from my nephew who was frantic with fear. He told me the city was about to be bombed from the air and advised me to get out of the building at once. I turned on the radio and heard the broadcast which corroborated what my nephew had said, grabbed my hat and coat and a few personal belongings and ran to the elevator. When I got to the street there were hundreds of people milling around in panic. Most of us ran toward Broadway and it was not until we stopped taxi drivers who had heard the entire broadcast on their radios that we knew what it was all about. It was the most asinine stunt I ever heard of.'

'I heard that broadcast and almost had a heart attack,' said Louis Winkler of Clay Avenue, the Bronx. 'I didn't tune it in until the programme was half over, but when I heard the names and titles of Federal, State and municipal officials and when the 'Secretary of the Interior' was introduced, I was convinced it was the McCoy. I ran out into the street with scores of others, and found people running in all directions. The whole thing came over as a news broadcast and in my mind it was a pretty crummy thing to do.'

The Telegraph Bureau switchboard at police headquarters in Manhattan, operated by thirteen men, was so swamped with calls from apprehensive citizens inquiring about the broadcast that police business was seriously interfered with.

Headquarters, unable to reach the radio station by telephone, sent a radio patrol car there to ascertain the reason for the reaction to the programme. When the explanation was given, a police message was sent to all precincts in the five boroughs advising the commands of the cause.

### 'They're Bombing New Jersey!'

Patrolman John Morrison was on duty at the switchboard in the Bronx Police Headquarters when, as he afterward expressed it, all the lines became busy at once. Among the first who answered was a man who informed him:

'They're bombing New Jersey!'

'How do you know?' Patrolman Morrison inquired.

'I heard it on the radio,' the voice at the other end of the wire replied. 'Then I went to the roof and I could see the smoke from the bombs, drifting over toward New York. What shall I do?'

The patrolman calmed the caller as well as he could, then answered other inquiries from persons who wanted to know whether the reports of a bombardment were true, and if so where they should take refuge.

At Brooklyn police headquarters, eight men assigned to the monitor switchboard estimated that they had answered more than 800 inquiries from persons who had been alarmed by the broadcast. A number of these, the police said, came from motorists who had heard the program over their car radios and were alarmed both for themselves and for persons at their homes. Also, the Brooklyn police reported, a preponderance of the calls seemed to come from women.

The National Broadcasting Company reported that men stationed at the WJZ transmitting station at Bound Brook, NJ, had received dozens of calls from residents of that area. The transmitting station communicated with New York and passed the information that there was no cause for alarm to the persons who inquired later.

Meanwhile the New York telephone operators of the company found their switchboards swamped with incoming demands for information, although the NBC system had no part in the programme.

*Record Westchester Calls*

The State, county, parkway and local police in Westchester Counter were swamped also with calls from terrified residents. Of the local police departments, Mount Vernon, White Plains, Mount Kisco, Yonkers and Tarrytown received most of the inquiries. At first the authorities thought they were being made the victims of a practical joke, but when the calls persisted and increased in volume they began to make inquiries. The New York Telephone Company reported that it had never handled so many calls in one hour in years in Westchester.

One man called the Mount Vernon Police Headquarters to find out 'where the forty policemen were killed'; another said his brother was ill in bed listening to the broadcast and when he heard the reports he got into an automobile and 'disappeared'. 'I'm nearly crazy!' the caller exclaimed.

Because some of the inmates took the catastrophic reports seriously as they came over the radio, some of the hospitals and the county penitentiary ordered that the radios be turned off.

Thousands of calls came in to Newark Police Headquarters. These were not only from the terrorstricken. Hundreds of physicians and nurses, believing the reports to be true, called to volunteer their services to aid the 'injured'. City officials also called in to make 'emergency' arrangements for the population. Radio cars were stopped by the panicky throughout that city.

Jersey City police headquarters received similar calls. One woman asked detective Timothy Grooty, on duty there, 'Shall I close my windows?' A man asked, 'Have the police any extra gas masks?' Many of the callers, on being assured the reports were fiction, queried again and again, uncertain in whom to believe.

Scores of persons in lower Newark Avenue, Jersey City, left their homes and stood fearfully in the street, looking with apprehension toward the sky. A radio car was dispatched there to reassure them.

The incident at Hedden Terrace and Hawthorne Avenue, in Newark, one of the most dramatic in the area, caused a tie-up in traffic for blocks around. The more than twenty families there apparently believed the 'gas attack' had started, and so reported to the police. An ambulance, three radio cars and a police emergency squad of eight men were sent to the scene with full inhalator apparatus.

They found the families with wet cloths on faces contorted with hysteria. The police calmed them, halted those who were attempting to move their furniture on their cars and after a time were able to clear the traffic snarl.

At St Michael's Hospital, High Street and Central Avenue, in the heart of the Newark industrial district, fifteen men and women were treated for shock and hysteria. In some cases it was necessary to give sedatives, and nurses and physicians sat down and talked with the more seriously affected.

While this was going on, three persons with children under treatment in the institution telephoned that they were taking them out and leaving the city, but their fears were calmed when hospital authorities explained what had happened.

A flickering of electric lights in Bergen County from about 6.15 to 6.30 last evening provided a build-up for the terror that was to ensue when the radio broadcast started.

Without going out entirely, the lights dimmed and brightened alternately and radio reception was also affected. The Public Service Gas and Electric Company was mystified by the behavior of the lights, declaring there was nothing wrong at their power plants or in their distributing system. A spokesman for the service department said a call was made to Newark and the same situation was reported. He believed, he said, that the condition was general throughout the state.

The New Jersey Bell Telephone Company reported that every central office in the state was flooded with calls for more than an hour and the company did not have time to summon emergency operators to relieve the congestion. Hardest hit was the Trenton toll office, which handled calls from all over the East.

One of the radio reports, the statement about the mobilization of 7,000 national guardsmen in New Jersey, caused the armories of the Sussex and Essex troops to be swamped with calls from officers and men seeking information about the mobilization place.

*Prayers for Deliverance*

In Caldwell, NJ, an excited parishioner ran into the First Baptist Church during evening services and shouted that a meteor had fallen, showering death and destruction, and that North Jersey was threatened. The Rev. Thomas Thomas, the pastor, quieted the congregation and all prayed for deliverance from the 'catastrophe'.

East Orange police headquarters received more than 200 calls from persons who wanted to know what to do to escape the 'gas'. Unaware of the broadcast, the switchboard operator tried to telephone Newark, but was unable to get the call through because the switchboard at Newark headquarters was tied up. The mystery was not cleared up until a Teletype explanation had been received from Trenton.

More than 100 calls were received at Maplewood police headquarters and during the excitement two families of motorists, residents of New York City, arrived at the station to inquire how they were to get back to their homes now that the Pulaski Skyway had been blown up.

The women and children were crying and it took some time for the police to convince them that the catastrophe was fictitious. Many persons who called Maplewood said their neighbors were packing their possessions and preparing to leave for the country.

In Orange, NJ, an unidentified man rushed into the lobby of the Lido Theatre, a neighborhood motion picture house, with the intention of 'warning' the audience that a meteor had fallen on Raymond Boulevard, Newark, and was spreading poisonous gases. Skeptical, Al Hochberg, manager of the theatre, prevented the man from entering the auditorium of the theatre and then called the police. He was informed that the radio broadcast was responsible for the man's alarm.

Emanuel Priola, bartender of a tavern at 442 Valley Road, West Orange, closed the place, sending away six customers, in the middle of the broadcast to 'rescue' his wife and two children.

'At first I thought it was a lot of Buck Rogers stuff, but when a friend telephoned me that general orders had been issued to evacuate everyone from the metropolitan area I put the customers out, closed the place and started to drive home,' he said.

William H. Decker of 20 Aubrey Road, Montclair, NJ, denounced the broadcast as 'a disgrace' and 'an outrage', which he said had frightened hundreds of residents in his community, including children. He said he knew of one woman who ran into the street with her two children and asked for the help of neighbours in saving them.

'We were sitting in the living room casually listening to the radio,' he said, 'when we heard reports of a meteor falling near New Brunswick and reports that gas was spreading. Then there was an announcement of the Secretary of Interior from Washington who spoke of the happening as a major disaster. It was the worst thing I ever heard over the air.'

*Columbia Explains Broadcast*

The Columbia Broadcasting System issued a statement saying that the adaptation of Mr Wells' novel which was broadcast 'followed the original closely, but to make the imaginary details more interesting to American listeners the adapter, Orson Welles, substituted an American locale for the English scenes of the story'.

Pointing out that the fictional character of the broadcast had been announced four times and had been previously publicized, it continued:

'Nevertheless, the programme apparently was produced with such vividness that some listeners who may have heard only fragments thought the broadcast was fact, not fiction. Hundreds of telephone calls reaching CBS stations, city authorities, newspaper offices and police headquarters in various cities testified to the mistaken belief.

'Naturally, it was neither Columbia's nor the Mercury Theatre's intention to mislead anyone, and when it became evident that a part of the audience had been disturbed by the performance five announcements were read over the network later in the evening to reassure those listeners.'

Expressing profound regret that his dramatic efforts should cause such consternation, Mr Welles said: 'I don't think we will choose anything like this again.' He hesitated about presenting it, he disclosed, because 'it was our thought that perhaps people might be bored or annoyed at hearing a tale so improbable'.

But it was *Time* magazine that came closest to the truth of why so many people were panicked into believing that their world was coming to an end on 30 October. In the 7 November 1938 edition, the magazine declared:

The only explanation for the badly panicked thousands – who evidently had neither given themselves the pleasure of familiarising themselves with Wells' famous book nor had the wit to confirm or deny the catastrophe by dialing another station – is that recent concern over a possible European Armageddon has badly spooked the American public.

It should also be remembered that at the time, nothing like *War of the Words* had ever been broadcast in the way presented by *The Mercury Theatre on the Air*. In 1938 people were still unsure about how to approach the new radio medium that was increasingly dominating the distribution of news and information. Since radio was the first electronic mass media, the public had widespread access to it in their homes. At the time, few inventions were comparable to the radio (unlike television, which came along well after the debates concerning radio's place in society). When viewed in this context, it is easier to understand how people might be fooled by a medium still in its infancy.

# CHAPTER TEN

# Meanwhile, Back at Grover's Mill

*'It would not have been a good idea for Orson Welles to have shown up,*
*I can tell you!'*
—*Grover's Mill resident on the day after the broadcast, October 1938*

The good people of Grover's Mill were very unhappy. Like thousands of others, some of the tiny hamlet's citizens had also tuned into *The Mercury Theatre on the Air*, only to hear that creatures from outer space had landed in their backyard. Those who believed that men from Mars had crash-landed near their homes gingerly peered out of windows to catch a glimpse of the invaders for themselves. But they saw nothing, and this puzzled them. There was only one Grover's Mill in New Jersey.

When the radio told them that state troopers were heading towards the Wilmuth Farm and the place where the giant meteor had come to rest, they knew that something was wrong. There wasn't a Wilmuth Farm in Grover's Mill – but there *was* a Wilson Farm. They calculated that the radio people had misheard the name.

Slowly and carefully, the farmers of Grover's Mill opened their front doors and crept outside onto their foggy front porches after giving wives and children orders to remain inside. One of them, Sam Dyce, said, 'Gosh damn, I'm going after my shotgun.' He ran back inside to take his weapon down from the wall. The others squinted through the misty darkness and saw flashlights moving through the gloom in the hands of their neighbours. Now that a dozen or so of Grover's Mill's finest were walking together towards Wilson Farm, the Martians had no chance of conquering any part of Mercer County. No sir!

Someone signalled for them to stop and nobody said a word. They stood in front of a large farmhouse and sure enough, towering above the back of the building they could just about see a 60-foot-tall spidery invader standing motionless and peering down on them. Sam Dyce raised his double-barrel shotgun and blasted the monster. There was a metallic sound as Mr Dyce's buckshot peppered the creature. And then another man reminded the shootist that he had just fired into a neighbour's old water tower – a tall wooden structure holding a huge water butt and mounted on top of metal legs. 'Better to be sure,' muttered Mr Dyce firmly, clenching his pipe between his teeth. 'You can never be too careful when it comes to aliens.'

They crept away as water began leaking from splintered buckshot holes, and made their way towards the flour mill and the large mill pond, where they expected to find the invaders rearing up towards them.

Close to the pond they heard tapping sounds. Someone said it was probably the Martians assembling their giant weapons of destruction. But it was nothing of the kind. Instead of finding terrifying aliens they discovered more neighbours, along with Arthur Buddington, chairman of Princeton University's geology department, and Professor Harry Hess, a geological expert in mineralogy. Armed with geologist's hammers and flashlights, they had rushed over to Grover's Mill with a handful of students before the programme had ended, hoping to find the meteor while it was still hot. As soon as they arrived they began tapping rocks to determine if they were of earthly or heavenly origin.

The question now was: what to do next? As it turned out, they did what all intrepid Grover's Millers do when alien invaders land in the neighbourhood but cannot be found. They all went home to bed.

Thanks to Welles and company, however, other Grover's Millers were wide awake. One man woke his children and he and his wife carried them to the car in order to escape to her family in Pennsylvania. But they were in such a hurry to get away from the space invaders that they forgot to open their garage doors and the car smashed through them. 'Never mind,' said the man of the house. 'We won't be needing those anymore.'

Early next morning, Grover's Mill was invaded by aliens of another kind – the American media. Reporters, photographers and newsreel cameramen began arriving before the farmers were up to milk the cows. They wanted to be taken to the very spot where the 'Martians' were said to have landed in the play. 'Were you scared? Did you really think aliens had landed in your township? Did any of you think you had seen anything strange? What do you think this 'alien invasion' might do for Grover's Mill? Do you have any message for Mr Orson Welles?'

Sam Dyce told a reporter, 'Everyone seemed to be suffering from hallucinations brought on by stark-naked fear. We got up to the lake and all we could see were people. It would not have been a good idea for Orson Welles to have shown up, I can tell you!'

The questions went on right through the day until early evening. And just when you thought you had dealt with one reporter, along came another and another – all asking the same damn fool questions. 'Of course we weren't taken in by the broadcast,' they said. 'There ain't no such thing as men from Mars, we didn't see nothin' – we were too busy listening to Charley McCarthy. If Orson Welles were to drive into Grover's Mill right now, I'd sure like to give him a piece of my mind, that's for sure, mister.'

A photograph of Grover's Mill veteran Bill Dock holding his rabbit gun appeared in *Life* magazine and for a few days he became a local hero. (© *Bettmann/CORBIS*)

Star of the media circus was seventy-six-year-old farmer Bill Dock, who was persuaded to take his rabbit shotgun down and pose for photographs next to a pile of grain sacks – pretending to be ready to repel any Martians that might be coming his way. His picture later appeared in *Life* magazine, and for a few days he was a local celebrity.

Fifty years after the panic broadcast, Bill Denison, whose father owned the eighteenth-century flour mill around which Grover's Mill had grown, still vividly remembered the evening of 30 October 1938:

We listened to a small part of the programme on the car radio while driving over to New Brunswick – but we didn't hear enough to recognise anything unusual. I went home that night and didn't think anything more about it until my father and I went to work at the mill the next morning and the radio was full of this great thing. People from all over the world were excited, particularly around the eastern part of the United States, because of the fantasy of the Martians landing at Grover's Mill. We couldn't operate that day at the mill because of the newspaper reporters and sightseers coming to see the mill, which looked exactly the same as it does today. It was the first time that I had seen an airplane taking aerial photographs. The New York newspapers were sending planes to take photos of where the Martians had landed. All the New York and Philadelphia reporters were there. People were there all day long just to see if there were any remnants of the Martians still there. One newspaper person even built a miniature rocket and stuck it in the ground, where it made a lot of smoke, and he said that's where the rocket came in. I didn't realise how major a story it was until years later.

While we were listening to the radio driving to New Brunswick, we hadn't heard any disclaimer that it was not a real story. And we didn't hear enough of it to understand that the Martians were landing, either. My parents didn't know about it, either. In fact, all the people who I associated with that night hadn't heard about it. Later I heard there were several people who tried to get out of town that night. I was told that one man who heard the show got so excited that he got his wife and kids into the car and went to the gas station to get gas and started down the road but ran out of gas. In his excitement, he had pumped all the gas onto the ground!

Much later I heard that one of Orson Welles' radio team had been in Princeton, but had not been to Grover's Mill, and chose the location by sticking a pin in a map. I tried to contact Orson Welles a few years later, but he had just left town and I didn't try to contact him again. His was a brilliant mind and I'm sorry that I didn't get a chance to talk with him.

Bill's wife Rachel heard the programme at home in Georgia. She recalled:

My father called everyone to the radio and said that the Martians were going to land in New Jersey. We were just glued to the radio. Later on, we realized that it wasn't true. Do you know that Bill and I never talked about this story and one day I was up in the attic at his mother's house in Grover's Mill and I found newspaper after newspaper with the story of the Martians landing in her community?

The programme brought unwanted fame to Grover's Mill. Bill remembers that after the war he was in Honshu, Japan, and was in a newspaper office where he told some people where he was from. 'They knew all about the *War of the Worlds* story. In 1988, on the fiftieth anniversary of the broadcast, CBS, NBC and Mutual Broadcast called me for a 'phone interview. It's amazing how many times I've told total strangers about *The War of the Worlds* and owning Grover's Mill.'

Shortly after the broadcast, while Bill's sister was working in a New York office, he called in to take her to lunch. 'I saw my picture was on the front page of one of those tabloid newspapers,' he remembered, 'and some of the girls in the office came up to her and said, "Isn't that your brother?" She said, "My gosh, it is." And that was my fifteen minutes of fame – no, make that two seconds; I couldn't stand fifteen minutes' worth!'

Sixty-three years after the famous broadcast, Grover's Mill resident Mabel Dey – who was sixteen years old when the Martians did not actually land in

**THE MEN FROM MARS**

Globe-Democrat Collection
St. Louis Mercantile Library

## ''HELP! MEN FROM MARS!''

FROM TIME TO TIME some quirk of fate, some state of mind, or some brilliance of thought makes a broadcast memorable. As such it deserves to be preserved, for after it passes from the news it becomes part of the color and woof of our history. As history and as a commentary on the nervous state of our nation after the Pact of Munich, we present this recent but none-the-less celebrated broadcast.

*Above and opposite:* Newspaper cartoonists across America had a fun-filled field day thanks to the broadcast. (*Radio Digest*; *St Louis Mercantile Library*; *Globe Democrat Collection*)

New Jersey – still remembers that foggy night before the name of Grover's Mill found its way into newspapers around the world.

On that night Mabel was at church playing the piano. 'Someone, I think it was a fella, came barging in and started shouting, "Martians have landed at Grover's Mill!" Well, I was learning about Hitler in school then, and I thought – and I know this sounds crazy – maybe Hitler and the Martians had gotten together, and this was the end of the world. So I stopped playing the piano, and I just bowed my head, and I prayed to the Lord.'

Mabel recalls how truly terrified she was that October night. It was the night that taught a young teenager to be forever wary of what she heard coming from the radio. 'All I could think in the church that night was that my mother was home alone,' she remembers. 'And if this was the end of the world, I wanted to be with her.'

\* \* \*

Other towns and villages near Grover's Mill also found their way into national and local newspapers. In Hamilton Township, close to the New Jersey Turnpike, it was reported that a woman had stuffed all her doors and windows with newspaper and wet rags before screaming to a policeman down the telephone, 'Fumes are already seeping into my living room. Help! What must I do?'

In the well-heeled area of Clinton Hill in Newark, New Jersey's largest city, police found over twenty families huddled together in the streets, surrounded by their belongings, their faces covered with water-soaked handkerchiefs. Fifteen of the group were treated for shock at St Michael's Hospital.

One man was treated at Mercer Hospital for a heart attack, which attendants said 'might possibly have been induced by the ultra-realistic broadcast'.

And then there were those who actually 'saw' the alien invaders with their own eyes and later described what they saw in minute detail. Trenton police received a call from a hysterical girl living close to Grover's Mill. 'You can't understand the horror of it,' she cried. 'It's hell.' Another man claimed that after hearing about the Martian attack, he climbed onto his roof, 'from where I could see the smoke from the bombs drifting. What shall I do?'

In Wood Bridge a terrified man, dragging his children behind him, burst into a church supper to grab his wife so they could all flee to safety together, while in nearby Orange, a man burst into a cinema crying, 'The state is being invaded. This place is going to be blown up.' Elsewhere in Orange, diners at a restaurant that had turned the radio on after the programme had started fled in terror – without waiting to pay their bills.

A woman ran into a church, screaming, 'New York is being destroyed; it's the end of the world. You might as well go home to die. I just heard it over the radio.' The congregation was dismissed immediately and they hurried back to their homes to prepare for Judgement Day.

While the invading Martians were still a long way from California, one excited man called the Oakland police telephone operator and shouted, 'My God! Where can I volunteer my services? We've got to stop this awful thing!'

In Macon, Georgia, a man listening to the play in a hospital bed while recovering from a major operation leapt up, tearing his stitches loose, and collapsed, while in Pittsburgh a man entered his house in the middle of the broadcast to find his wife clutching a bottle of poison and screaming, 'I'd rather die this way than like that.'

In later years, Welles would recall the many different ways the American public had reacted that night. His favourite was about the actor John Barrymore, who was tuned into the show. Said Welles, 'Although he was a friend of mine, he ceased to identify me with the show and believed implicitly that America had fallen to the Martians. And hearing this on his radio, he put down his highball and rushed out to his backyard, where he kept ten Great Danes in private kennels. He released the dogs, crying to them as they ran in all directions, "The world has fallen, fend for yourselves!"'

Welles related other stories generated by the broadcast on the many talk shows he appeared in both the United States and Britain over the next thirty-five years. In one of them, he claimed that ships from the US Naval fleet had earlier in the day anchored in the Port of New York and their crews were given shore leave. Once it had been announced that invaders from another planet had landed in New Jersey, they were immediately recalled to their ships so that they might sail out in readiness to repel the aliens approaching the city. In the years that followed, countless sailors recalled that night and told Welles how he had ruined the first decent shore leave they had had in months.

He also liked to tell the story of a smart and exclusive Long Island dinner party taking place on the night of the broadcast:

> Lots of grand people were sitting at dinner, and about halfway through, the butler arrived to serve the next course, and said to the host, in an undertone, which carried around the table, 'I beg pardon, sir, but New Jersey has just fallen.' Everyone was very contained and polite... Nobody panicked.
>
> They waited till the next course, and the butler came around again, and the host said, 'Meadows,' or whatever his name was, 'what was that you said, Meadows, where did you hear that?'
>
> 'On the radio, sir.'
>
> 'Exactly what happened?'
>
> 'Well, I believe sir, that the greater part of the Atlantic seaboard has capitulated.'
>
> Of course, everybody assumed it must be the communists or something. By the time the baked Alaska came, the host said, 'Meadows, hum... Have you ascertained who it is that's attacking us?'
>
> 'I believe it's interplanetary, sir.'
>
> At this point, according to my informant, who is highly placed and should be believed, they looked out the window, and there was a falling star. Now I can't vouch for that part of the story, but anyway that's what was told.

Welles also claimed he had been told by a former Red Cross official working in the Kentucky hillbilly country that, on hearing that Martians had invaded America, entire families fled into the mountains and refused to come out for six weeks.

Such was the power of radio.

CHAPTER ELEVEN

# Jitterbugs and Crackpots

*'I suppose that by this time you have received many letters from numerous cranks and crackpots who quickly became jitterbugs during the programme. I was one of the thousands who heard the programme … and sat serenely entertained no end by the fine portrayal of a fine play.'*
—*A 'satisfied radio listener' from South Dakota*

According to Howard Koch, the fates of everyone who had participated in the panic broadcast 'hung in the balance' the morning after the show went on air. Network executives met in secret to discuss whether they were proud or ashamed of what had been broadcast live over their airwaves the previous evening.

There was talk of the radio series being cancelled with immediate effect 'in the public interest'. Others suggested that CBS might have its licence revoked, putting hundreds of actors, technicians, musicians and clerical staff out of work and causing the network's shares to plummet. Welles became the media's whipping boy and newspapers across the land published angry letters from listeners demanding that he should never again be allowed to stand in front of a microphone. There was also talk of criminal action amounting to over $12 million being taken for damages, injuries and distress of various kinds.

Members of the Mercury Theatre, however, looked at the millions of pounds' worth of unbuyable publicity generated through the media and hoped that the event might, at best, give their careers a boost and assist box office business for *Danton's Death*. What Welles did not – could not – know at that time was that the 'hoax broadcast', as it came to be known, would make him 'notorious' forever in the eyes of theatre, radio and (shortly afterwards) cinema audiences across the world. Over seventy years after *The War of the Worlds* was originally unleashed on an unsuspecting world, it is one of the most memorable radio broadcasts ever made. People still talk about it. Academics and students of mass communication theorise about it. Several books have even been written about it.

Hundreds of listeners ran to their lawyers threatening to sue CBS in general – and Orson Welles in particular. They claimed that arms had been broken while they rushed panic-stricken from their homes. They had fallen down the stairs and were unable to work for a week, meaning they lost a week's pay. Other listeners said that thanks to Orson Welles they had smashed their car during the stampede to escape from invading Martians. Damages were sought from women claiming they had suffered miscarriages as a result of the broadcast. Others said they planned to sue the network for 'distress', while a man in Chicago claimed that his wife 'and several other women he knew' had been 'confined to their beds from shock and hysteria' caused by the radio play.

An actress from Los Angeles called Sara Collins filed a $50,000 damage lawsuit in the superior court against CBS, claiming she had 'suffered from nervous shock while listening to the broadcast'. Attorney Oliver M. Hickey said Miss Collins believed that what she was hearing on the radio was true and actually occurring. The actress told her attorney that CBS, like other radio networks, often sent out news bulletins 'and that she had no reason to believe the broadcast she heard was untrue'.

Miss Collins was pictured in Los Angeles newspapers wearing her best hat and coat, her hands 'raised in shock', presumably reproducing the gesture she had made while listening to her radio that Sunday.

Los Angeles actress Sara Collins filed a $50,000 damage lawsuit in the Superior Court against CBS, claiming she 'suffered from nervous shock' while listening to *The War of the Worlds*. (*Los Angeles Herald-Express*)

Welles would later lament that the papers had made up the lawsuit headlines because of their competitive envy of radio advertising. But Welles never questioned the extent of the panic or the newspapers' coverage of the event outside of the lawsuit stories.

Houseman later said that of the lawsuits brought against CBS, the Mercury Theatre and Orson Welles, none were substantiated or legally proved and that the only people who profited were scores of lawyers across the United States. 'We did settle one claim, however, against the advice of our lawyers,' wrote Houseman. 'It was the particularly affecting case of a man in Massachusetts who, after hearing that aliens had landed on his side of the USA, wrote: "I thought the best thing to do was to go away. So I took $3.25 out of my savings and bought a ticket. After I had gone sixty miles I knew it was a play. Now I don't have money left for the shoes I was saving up for. Will you please have someone send me a pair of black shoes size 9B?"'

And Houseman did.

* * *

There were demands for a full investigation while officials at the Harvard astronomical observatory calmed fears of a conquest from space with the wry comment that there was 'no evidence of higher life existing on Mars, some 40,000,000 miles distant'.

On the morning after the broadcast, the US Federal Communications Commission (FCC), an independent government agency set up four years previously to regulate communications by radio, hastily convened a meeting in Washington to discuss the crisis. The FCC had clearly been caught off guard by the play, which became the first case – and, to date, the only case – brought before it in which a single fictional broadcast had detonated nationwide panic.

Frank Ramsay McNinch was a sixty-six-year-old former mayor of the city of Charlotte, North Carolina, whom President Franklin Roosevelt had plucked from his job as head of the Federal Power Commission and made chairman of the turbulent FCC. McNinch's brief was to launch a radio 'clean-up job', which was supposed to last about three months, but the FCC had become more turbulent than ever following increasing numbers of complaints about what went over the American airwaves and into the homes of millions of citizens.

McNinch called the members of the commission together to discuss what – if anything – should be done in light of the fuss created by the media. CBS officials were also summoned to the capital and ordered to bring with them copies of *The War of the Worlds* scripts and a wax disc recording to play to the seven-man commission, most of whom has not heard the broadcast.

McNinch told the media, 'Any broadcast that creates such general panic and fear as this one is reported to have done is, to say the least, regrettable. I have received many telephone calls and telegrams about the broadcast.'

The future fate of CBS was in the hands of the US Federal Communications Commission, who discussed revoking the broadcaster's licence following the broadcast. Chairman Frank McNinch is seated centre, along with Eugene O. Sykes (left) and Paul A. Walker (right). Back row (left to right) are T. A. M. Craven, Thad. A. Brown, Norman S. Case and George Henry Payne. (*Author's collection*)

In total the Commission had received over 600 letters about the programme, 60 per cent of them complaining and insisting that Orson Welles be punished in some way and other members of the cast be disciplined. Here are just two of the letters, the first an angry communication from Paul Morton, city manager of Trenton, New Jersey. It was boldly headed, 'COMPLAINT – WABC BROADCAST.' It read:

> Gentlemen: To avoid a reoccurrence of a very grave and serious situation that developed in this community last night, due to the public's misinterpretation of the broadcast through WABC at about 8.15, dramatizing H. G. Wells' *The War of the Worlds*, which completely crippled communication facilities of our Police Department for about three hours, I am requesting that you immediately make an investigation and do everything possible to prevent a reoccurrence.
>
> The situation was so acute that two thousand phone calls were received in about two hours, all communication lines were paralyzed and voided normal municipal functions. If we had had a large fire at this time it could have easily

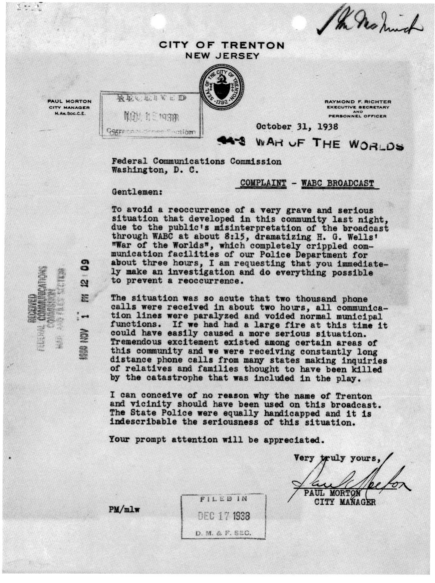

**CITY OF TRENTON**
**NEW JERSEY**

PAUL MORTON
CITY MANAGER
M.AM.SOC.C.E.

RECEIVED
NOV 1 5 1938

RAYMOND F. RICHTER
EXECUTIVE SECRETARY
AND
PERSONNEL OFFICER

October 31, 1938

44-3 WAR OF THE WORLDS

Federal Communications Commission
Washington, D. C.

<u>COMPLAINT - WABC BROADCAST</u>

Gentlemen:

To avoid a reoccurrence of a very grave and serious
situation that developed in this community last night,
due to the public's misinterpretation of the broadcast
through WABC at about 8:15, dramatizing H. G. Wells'
"War of the Worlds", which completely crippled communication facilities of our Police Department for
about three hours, I am requesting that you immediately make an investigation and do everything possible
to prevent a reoccurrence.

The situation was so acute that two thousand phone
calls were received in about two hours, all communication lines were paralyzed and voided normal municipal
functions. If we had had a large fire at this time it
could have easily caused a more serious situation.
Tremendous excitement existed among certain areas of
this community and we were receiving constantly long
distance phone calls from many states making inquiries
of relatives and families thought to have been killed
by the catastrophe that was included in the play.

I can conceive of no reason why the name of Trenton
and vicinity should have been used on this broadcast.
The State Police were equally handicapped and it is
indescribable the seriousness of this situation.

Your prompt attention will be appreciated.

Very truly yours,

PAUL MORTON
CITY MANAGER

PM/mlw

FILED IN
DEC 17 1938
D. M. & F. SEC.

RECEIVED
FEDERAL COMMUNICATIONS COMMISSION
MAIL AND FILES SECTION
1938 NOV 1 PM 12 09

*Above and opposite:* For and against *The War of the Worlds.* Letters to the Federal
Communications Commission expressing both anger and pleasure. (*The National
Archives and Records Administration*)

Aberdeen, S. Dak.
November 1, 1938

Federal Communications Commission
Washington, D. C.

44-8 WAR OF THE WOR 5S

Gentlemen:

      I have read considerable concerning the program of Orson Welles presented over the Columbia Broadcasting System Sunday evening. I suppose that by this time you have received many letters from numerous cranks and crack-pots who quickly became jitterbugs during the program. I was one of the thousands who heard this program and did not jump out of the window, did not attempt suicide, did not break my arm while beating a hasty retreat from my apartment, did not anticipate a horrible death, did not hear the Martians "rapping on my chamber door", did not see the monsters landing in war-like regalia in the park across the street, but sat serenely entertained no end by the fine portrayal of a fine play.

      The "Mercury Theatre" has been one of the radio high-lights of the week for me this fall. The program Sunday, I felt, was one of their better programs.

      Should your commission contemplate serious measures toward the Columbia Broadcasting System my suggestion would be that the "Mercury Theatre" be directed to re-broadcast this program and the reaction of all the listening audience be solicited.

      In the interest of a continuation of the fine things in radio today, I am,

                Very respectfully yours,

                J. V. Yaukey

FILED IN
DEC 15 1938
D. M. & F. SEC.

P.S.- I am in the State Administrative office of the South Dakota State Employment Service and every member of our staff who heard the program subscribes to what I have had to say.

caused a more serious situation. Tremendous excitement existed among certain areas of this community and we were receiving constantly long distance phone calls from many states making inquiries of relatives and families thought to have been killed by the catastrophe that was included in the play.

I can conceive of no reason why the name of Trenton and vicinity should have been used on this broadcast. The State Police were equally handicapped and it is indescribable the seriousness of this situation. Your prompt attention will be appreciated.

But not everyone wrote to the Commission to complain. Letters were also received from listeners who had enjoyed the broadcast and admired the Mercury's innovative approach to storytelling. The following letter from Mr J. D. Yaukey of Aberdeen, South Dakota, states:

Gentlemen: I have read considerable amounts concerning the programme of Orson Welles presented over the Columbia Broadcasting System on Sunday evening. I suppose that by this time you have received many letters from numerous cranks and crackpots who quickly became jitterbugs during the programme. I was one of the thousands who heard the programme and I did *not* jump out of the window, did *not* attempt suicide, did *not* break my arm while beating a hasty retreat from my apartment, did *not* anticipate a horrible death, did *not* hear the Martians 'rapping on my chamber door', did *not* see the monsters landing in war-like regalia in the park across the street, but sat serenely entertained no end by the fine portrayal of a fine play.

The Mercury Theatre has been one of the radio highlights of the week for me this fall. The programme Sunday, I felt, was one of their better programmes.

Should your commission contemplate serious measures towards the Columbia Broadcasting System my suggesting would be that the Mercury Theatre be directed to re-broadcast the programme and the reaction of all the listening audience so solicited.

In the interest of a continuation of the fine things in radio today, I am, very respectfully yours, J. V. Yaukey.

PS – I am in the State Administrative office of the South Dakota State Employment Service and every member of our staff who heard the programme subscribe to what I have had to say.

Popular American singer, comedian and radio star Eddie Cantor – known to millions by his nickname of 'Banjo Eyes' – fired off a telegram to commissioners urging them to consider the future of radio as public entertainment. He stated that *The Mercury Theatre on the Air*'s drama 'was a melodramatic masterpiece … censorship would retard radio immeasurably and produce a spineless radio theatre as unbelievable as the script of *The War of the Worlds*.'

One handwritten letter was received from a twelve-year old boy called Clifford Sickles from Rockford, Illinois, who told the commission, 'I enjoyed the broadcast of Mr Welles. I heard about half of it but my mother and sister got frightened and I had to turn it off.'

The editor's letters page of the influential *New York Times* also carried messages 'for' and 'against' *The War of the Worlds*. George Rutherford of New York wrote:

> The bad taste and lack of restraint in the Halloween 'joke' broadcast cannot be too harshly condemned. It would appear that radio is in incompetent hands if the studios lack persons with enough responsibility to prevent the sending of such frightfulness into the homes of a people already jittery from war talk, depression and political uncertainty.
>
> Make no mistake, it was not the ignorant, not the believers in ghosts, who took this thing seriously. It was those who, acquainted with our own scientific accomplishments, see nothing impossible in any dream of what a more advanced people out in space might be able to accomplish. Everyone connected with the broadcast showed complete lack of editorial discretion as well as a perverted sense of humour.

Maurice Calman of New York wrote:

> Vivid dramatizations over the radio of imaginary catastrophes, making use of names of actual person, towns, cities and States, as was done last night by station WABC ought to be prohibited by law.
>
> Should a real catastrophe take place, people may take it to be another hoax, in spite of urgent pleas by the authorities to the contrary.

On the other hand, Pat George of New York wrote:

> When daily newspapers, especially *The New York Times*, go to the trouble of publishing itemized reports of the daily radio programmes, the mass hysteria of Sunday evening is entirely uncalled for. It was just plain stupidity.

Alvin J. Bogart of Cranford, New Jersey commented:

> May we hope that no action will be taken against the Columbia Broadcasting System for the brilliant dramatization of H. G. Wells' fantasy *The War of the Worlds*?
>
> I was fortunate in having my attention called to the broadcast by an excited friend after the opening announcement of its fictional nature had been made, and thus could appreciate its realism to the hilt.
>
> Condemnation of the network for the childish hysteria and panic of the part of many listeners would place the Federal Communications Commission

on a par with those emotional and somewhat moronic individuals who, in shame at their own credulity and panic, are now indignant and vindictive.

Ruth Fleurnoy Bloomsburgh from Albany wrote to put 'ourselves on record as stranger than Martians in the now much-discussed radio drama'. She continued:

> We read our own radio programmes in the paper. We listen to and remember the announcements about coming attractions. We heard this announced and heard other announcements during the programme. We feel that we must not be too lazy to do our own censoring to suit our own needs. If we keep on asking for protection in the things in and of the world we live in, and refuse to do our own part in it, we will all be useless gibbering idiots through failure to stop our headline type of reading and waiting for someone to take care of us by forming our opinions.

George Bellamy from New York was brief and to the point:

> Unless the American average of intelligence is lower than some people suspect, I for one refuse to believe that any but children, old ladies and mental deficients were seriously perturbed by what struck my family and self merely as a boring and rather inane production.

The American people had spoken. Now it was up to the gentlemen of the US Federal Communications Commission to make up their own minds what to do.

\* \* \*

When the commissioners sat around their Washington table, they came to the conclusion that the law conferred upon it no regulatory power over broadcasting content. They agreed that while certain specific offences, such as obscenity, were forbidden – as in the notorious case against Mae West and her appearance on *The Chase and Sanborn Hour* the previous year – there was strong opposition to using 'the public interest' clause to impose programme restrictions. The commission was 'particularly outspoken against anything resembling censorship', stating that it 'should make no attempt at censoring what shall or shall not be said over the radio'. Mr McNinch said, 'The public does not want a spineless radio.'

Commissioner George Payne, however, stated that radio was an entirely different medium from the theatre or lecture platform, adding, 'People who have material broadcast into their homes without warnings have a right to protection. Too many broadcasters have insisted that they could broadcast anything they liked, contending that they were protected by the prohibition of censorship. Certainly when people are injured morally, physically, spiritually and psychically, they have just as much right to complain as if the laws against obscenity and indecency were violated.'

CBS – which received 1,770 assorted letters, 1,086 of them complementary and the rest criticising the programme – called attention to the fact that on the night of the broadcast it had assured listeners that the story was wholly imaginary, and W. B. Lewis, vice president in charge of programmes, stated, 'In order that this may not happen again, the programme department hereafter will not use the technique of a stimulated news broadcast within a dramatisation when the circumstances of the broadcast could cause immediate alarm to numbers of listeners.'

The National Association of Broadcasters, through its president, Neville Miller, expressed formal regret for the misinterpretation of the programme. 'I know that CBS and those of us in radio have only the most profound regret that the composure of many of our fellow citizens was disturbed by the vivid Orson Welles broadcast.'

Two weeks later McNinch delivered a speech to the National Association of Broadcasters convention, suggesting that the best guidance on programme standards 'should come from the public opinion of the listeners, rather than the broadcasters or the commission'. He stressed that broadcast station licensees were in the position of trustees, with the American public being the fiduciaries of the trust. All major networks – including CBS – carried the speech live over the radio.

The FCC completed its formal investigation into *The War of the Worlds* just over one month from the date of the broadcast. On 5 December 1938, a press release regarding its decision on the matter was issued:

> The FCC announced today that in its judgment steps taken by CBS since the Orson Welles *Mercury Theatre on the Air* programme on October 30 are sufficient to protect the public interest. Accordingly complaints received regarding this programme will not be taken into account in considering the renewals of licenses of stations carrying the broadcast.
>
> The FCC stated that, while it is regrettable that the broadcast alarmed a substantial number of people, there appeared to be no likelihood of a repetition of the incident and no occasion for action by the FCC. In reaching this determination, the FCC had before it a statement by Mr W. B. Lewis, Vice President in charge of programmes of the CBS, expressing regret that some listeners 'mistook fantasy for fact' and saying in part, 'In order that this may not happen again, the Programme Department hereafter will not use the technique of a simulated news broadcast within a dramatization when the circumstances of the broadcast could cause immediate alarm to numbers of listeners.'

The FCC had also heard a transcript of the programme and had been informed regarding a number of communications concerning it. It was made known that the FCC received 372 protests against the broadcast, while 255 letters and petitions favoring it were received. Counting those who signed petitions, those who expressed themselves as favorable to the broadcast numbered approximately 350.

Everyone working in American radio breathed a collective sigh of relief that could be heard across the nation. CBS retained its licence, but went about its business as if it were treading on eggshells to avoid upsetting anyone. The staff of *The Mercury Theatre on the Air* were told they were naughty boys and must never allow anything like this to happen again, but could continue business as usual – and to expect record ratings when the following week's programme went on air.

The panic broadcast never really went away. Two years later, on 31 March 1940 – the eve of April Fools' Day – comedian Jack Benny in his popular Sunday evening NBC radio show held 'an imaginary telephone conversation' with Orson Welles, jokingly blaming recent sunspot magnetic storms on him and expressing worries about the end of the world. In Philadelphia, William A. A. Castellini of the Franklin Institute's Fels Planetarium telegraphed Benny, telling him, 'Your worst fears that world will end are confirmed by astronomers of the Franklin Institute. Scientists predict that the world will end at 3 p.m.'

A radio announcer read the telegram in a news broadcast following Benny's programme but made no mention of the comedian's sketch. The bulletin stated:

Your worst fears that the world will end are confirmed by astronomers at the Franklin Institute, Philadelphia. Scientists predict that the world will end at 3 p.m. Eastern Standard Time tomorrow. This is no April Fools' joke. Confirmation can be obtained from Wagner Schlesinger, director of the Fels Planetarium of this city.

Public reaction to the announcement was swift and dramatic. Philadelphia's newspapers, police stations and the city's information bureau received hundreds of calls from frightened citizens. The radio station later issued an apology and explanation, but denied responsibility for it. The station admitted it had received the announcement from William Castellini, a press agent for the Franklin Institute, and read it in good faith, believing it to be genuine. However, Castellini had intended it as a publicity gimmick to promote a 1 April lecture at the planetarium, titled 'How Will the World End?' Castellini later explained that he came up with his April Fools' Day idea after recalling the Mercury Theatre's panic broadcast. While hearing Jack Benny's show, he thought it might be a good idea to generate publicity for the planetarium. In his own defence he claimed that he had 'informed some of the people' at the radio station about the announcement and 'thought they would know it was a stunt'. He was later fired by the Franklin Institute.

* * *

Not everyone was happy with the aftermath of the Martian saga. Senator Clyde L. Herring of Iowa claimed that the drama 'was proof that radio needed control by the government'. The senator threatened that he was preparing a bill for the upcoming legislative session that would permit the commission to screen and veto every radio programme before broadcast. His statement represented one of the most unabashed calls for direct government control of the airwaves by an American official in the new electronic media age.

Senator Herring claimed that previous years had witnessed 'a rising chorus of criticism towards radio programming', described by many as being 'increasingly indecent and incendiary'. He was probably referring to Mae West's 'remarks' to Charlie McCarthy on *The Chase and Sanborn Hour.*

*The War of the Worlds* had unwittingly brought the debate concerning radio censorship to a level of intensity never before experienced in the United States. Despite often antagonistic relationships between newspapers and radio at the time, most print editorials tended to favour self-regulation. One of the more unequivocal editorials came from the *New York Daily News*, which received 191 letters 'and the bulk of these concerned Sunday evening's nationwide invasion from Mars radio scare'. It continued:

> Practically all our correspondents were in a rage when they wrote. About half of them were mad at the people who were hoaxed into taking the broadcast seriously; the other half were mad at Orson Welles, who put on the programme and for having done the job so vividly and convincingly.
>
> We can't get mad against either of these targets. The only parties to the excitement that we're mad at are the FCC for making such a fuss about it, and Senator Clyde L. Herring who has seized the incident as a pretext for renewing his drive for government radio censorship. We wish the FCC would relax and go back to sleep. We hope the next Congress, and as many Congresses thereafter as necessary, will smack flat all radio censorship bills with the avalanche of '*no's*' they deserve in a free-speech, free-press, free-religion, free-assemblage country.

Senator Herring's legislation was never adopted, although the panic broadcast did much to enhance the American public's awareness of the FCC, which had demonstrated that it had the power to close down a radio station if it really wanted to.

* * *

Hadley Cantril, an American public opinion researcher, commented that the situation created by *The War of the Worlds* showed 'how the common man reacts in a time of stress and strain. It gives us insights into his intelligence, his anxieties, his needs, which we could never get by tests or strictly experimental studies. The panic situation ... had all the flavour of everyday life and, at the same time, provided a semi-experimental condition for research.'

Lessons had certainly been learned. Following the fuss, there was talk of the broadcast being a planned conspiracy deliberately set up by the US Government to test the reaction of American radio listeners upon hearing news that interplanetary invaders had landed in their country. Some people today still believe the theory.

But in November 1938 Washington was abuzz with talk that following the coast-to-coast alarm, radio loudspeakers should be positioned in every public square in the United States to give out warnings – real or otherwise – of attacks by invaders of any kind.

What struck many listeners about the play was its immediate emotional effect on the public. Thousands of people had been convinced that a real invasion had been unleashed. They had exhibited all the symptoms of fear, panic, determination to resist, desperation, bravery, excitement and fatalism that a 'real invasion' might produce. Military experts declared that such widespread reactions demonstrated that the US Government 'would have to insist on the close co-operation of radio in any future war'.

This would be achieved through voluntary agreements among radio stations to 'refrain from over-dramatising war announcements, which would react on the public like Sunday night's fictional announcement'.

Because radio had such an immediate effect, experts believed that every American citizen should have access to facilities for listening in, should a war – or interplanetary invasion – happen for real.

Three years later, on 7 December 1941, the Imperial Japanese Navy dropped its deadly bombs onto American warships anchored in Pearl Harbor. War with Japan was declared and three days later the US was also at war with Germany. Millions heard the news through their radio sets. Loudspeaker systems in public squares were not needed. You had to have been living on Mars to not have known that things would never be the same again.*

---

* It is ironic, but true, that President Roosevelt later told Orson Welles personally that many thought his Pearl Harbour radio broadcast on 7 December 1941 was 'another Orson Welles hoax' designed to 'make people think that the country had gone to war'. On the morning of the attack Welles was broadcasting a live patriotic programme, which was interrupted to announce the Japanese attack.

# CHAPTER TWELVE

# In the Soup

*'We have far more to fear from the silhouette of the censor
than from the shadow of Orson Welles.'*
—*Haywood Broun,* New York World-Telegram, *November 1938*

The furore was still raging days after the Martians failed to destroy America, although other murmurs were heard above the shouts of the angry mob. And many of these murmurs were aimed directly at the censoring powers of the Federal Communications Commission and the gullibility of American people.

Influential columnists writing for leading newspapers began to see something other than shock/horror/fear/outrage in the broadcast. Hugh S. Johnson, a speechwriter for President Roosevelt, co-author of his New Deal and now a no-nonsense syndicated columnist with Scripps-Howard newspapers, thought the 'Mars panic' presented useful lessons for the American people.

Three days after the shock broadcast he wrote:

One of the most remarkable demonstrations of modern times was the startling effect of the absurd radio scenario by Orson Welles of *The War of the Worlds.* Simulated Columbia broadcast radio flashes of a pretended attack with mysterious new aerial weapons on New Jersey from the planet Mars put many people into such a panic that the Witch-burning Mr McNinch, Chairman of the Federal Communications Commission, has a new excuse to extend the creeping hand of government restrictions of free speech by way of radio censorship.

When the hysterical echoes of an initial hysterical explosion die down the whole incident will assay out as about the silliest teapot tempest in human history ... The result of public panic was so absurd as to be unpredictable by anybody – even CBS and the author of the script. The idea of using the incident to discipline or censor anybody is ridiculous.

But the incident is highly significant. It reveals dramatically a state of public mind. Too many people have been led by outright propaganda to believe in some new and magic power of air attack and other developments in the weapons of war ... If this hysterical happening means anything it is that there is a vague restless suspicion among the people of the truth that there has been such neglect.

Johnson wrote that the broadcast had demonstrated 'dramatic proof of the jitters of our own people on the subject of our own defenses', adding:

On the face of things a similar thing will not be permitted to happen again by any of our great broadcasting systems. But when the smoke all drifts away their innocence will be clear and the value of this incident may be credited to them as an unintended assistance to the President's great defence programme.

In another popular syndicated column, 'It Seems to Me', commentator Heywood Broun wrote in the *New York World-Telegram*:

I'm still scared. I didn't hear the broadcast and I doubt that I would have called up the police to complain merely because I heard that men from a strange machine were knocking the daylights out of Princeton. That doesn't happen to be news this season ... Just the same, I live in terror that almost any time now a metal cylinder will come to earth and out of it will step some fearsome creatures carrying death ray guns. And their faces will be forbidding, because the next radio invasion is likely to be an expedition to the censors.

Obviously, Orson Welles put too much curdle on the radio ways, but there isn't a chance on Earth than any chain will sanction such a stunt again. In fact, I think it would be an excellent rule to make the provision that nothing can be put forward as news broadcast unless it actually is news...

We have much more reason to fear censors than octopi from the distant skies. The weapons which they may use can be much more far-reaching and devastating than any to be conjured up in a fantastic horror story. It is not a good thing that thousands of gullible people should be needlessly frightened out of their wits, if any. Possibly it is too much to ask the mixed audiences which radio commands to face the inventions of that lively pseudo-scientific sort to which the imagination of H. G. Wells turned when he was very young...

Columnist and broadcaster Dorothy Thompson had been called 'one of the two most influential women in America'. The other was Eleanor Roosevelt, the wife of the president. In her 'On the Record' column in the *New York Tribune* on 2 November, Thompson observed:

All unwittingly Mr Orson Welles and *The Mercury Theatre on the Air* have made one of the most fascinating and important demonstrations of all time. They have proved that a few effective voices, accompanied by sound effects, can so convince masses of people of a totally unreasonable, completely fantastic proposition as to create nationwide panic.

They have demonstrated more potently than any argument, demonstrated beyond question of a doubt, the appalling dangers and enormous effectiveness of popular and theatrical demagoguery.

They have cast a brilliant and cruel light upon the failure of popular education.

They have shown up the incredible stupidity, lack of nerve and ignorance of thousands.

They have proved how easy it is to start a mass delusion. They have uncovered the primeval fears lying under the thinnest surface of the so-called civilised man. They have shown that man, when the victim of his own gullibility, turns to the government to protect him against his own errors of judgement.

The newspapers are correct in playing up this story over every other news event in the world. It is the story of the century. And far from blaming Mr Orson Welles, he ought to be given a Congressional medal and a national prize for having made the most amazing and important contribution to an understanding of Hitlerism, Mussolinism, Stalinism, anti-Semitism and all the other terrorisms of our times than all the words about them that have been written by reasonable men ... They have thrown more light on recent events in Europe leading to the Munich pact than everything that has been said on the subject by all the journalists and commentators.

Hitler managed to scare all Europe to its knees a month ago, but he at least had an army and an air force to back up his shrieking words. But Mr Welles scared thousands into demoralization with nothing at all. That historic hour on the air was an act of unconscious genius, performed by the very innocence of intelligence.

Thompson also wrote:

Nothing whatever about the dramatization of *The War of the Worlds* was in the least credible, no matter at what point the hearer might have tuned in. The entire verisimilitude was in the names of a few specific places. Monsters were depicted of a type that nobody has ever seen, equipped with 'rays' entirely fantastic; they were described as 'straddling the Pulaski Skyway' and throughout the broadcast they were referred to as Martians, men from another planet.

A twist of the dial would have established for anybody that the national catastrophe was not being noted on any other station. A second of logic would have dispelled any terror. A notice that the broadcast came from a non-existent agency would have awakened skepticism...

The time element was obviously lunatic. Listeners were told that 'within two hours 3 million people have moved out of New York' – an obvious impossibility for the most disciplined army moving exactly as planned and a double fallacy because, only a few minutes before, the news of the arrival of the monster had been announced.

And, of course, it was not even a planned hoax. Nobody was more surprised at the result than Mr Welles. The public was told at the beginning, at the end and during the course of the drama that it *was* a drama.

Thompson attacked the unwariness of the 'deceived' listening public who were 'furious and of course demanded that the state protect them, demonstrating that they were incapable of relying on their own judgement'.

Other columnists pointed out that 'the jumpy state of nerves brought on by the war clouds over Europe and Asia' had revealed how the episode had driven home 'how little prepared the nation is to cope with an abrupt emergency. Thus, it is being pointed out that CBS has inadvertently done a lot for national defence.'

News of the broadcasting furore found its way across the Atlantic to where British newspaper men were bothering H. G. Wells as much as the American media was bothering Orson Welles. Reports also reached the ears of Hitler's speechwriters. In a speech alluding to the broadcast and delivered to hundreds of people in Munich's Bürgerbräukeller in November 1938, Hitler said that the German people 'would not fall into the fear of bombs from Mars or the moon'.

Benito Mussolini's fascist daily paper, *Il Resto del Carlino*, told readers that 'the mythical Martians have put a third-rate democracy into tragic confusion'. Il Duce 'hailed the hysterical exhibition as a sign of the decadence and cowardice of American democracy'.

Joseph Goebbels, Hitler's Reich Minister for Public Enlightenment and Propaganda – who used the power of radio to inform German citizens that the upcoming war was a defensive measure to protect them from invading enemies – also heard about the famous American broadcast. In a front-page story published in his twice-weekly newspaper *Der Angriff* ('The Attack') on 2 November, an editorial stated:

> If Americans fall so easily for a fantastic radio broadcast of an invasion from Mars, that explains why they so readily believe Nazi atrocity tales … Naiveté is a gift of God, but it should not be abused … This explains a lot about the Old World.

On the same day a cartoon in *Das Schwarze Korps* ('The Black Corps'), the official newspaper of the SS, showed New York being invaded Martians. In accordance with official Nazi party doctrine, the cartoon implied that New York public life was dominated by rich Jews. One Martian says to the other: 'You're wrong, Kaster, we have not discovered America, but Palestine!'

\* \* \*

Thousands across the country who had missed the by now infamous programme were kicking themselves. The play and the effect it had had on the public was the topic of everybody's conversation for days. Most who had tuned in refused to admit they had been taken in by what they had heard. Others spoke about how realistic it had been thanks to the skilful acting and creepy sound effects. They said they would not have missed the show for the world – this one or any other.

Those who had missed the programme hoped that CBS might repeat it sometime soon. The network, knowing it would stage a ratings coup over just about every other programme broadcast at the same time, flatly refused even though five out of every six requests were from people who had missed it first time around. Much as CBS would have loved to repeat radio's most talked-about programme, they still feared that a small minority of American listeners who had not heard that the world nearly came to an end on 30 October might tune in and thus trigger off a repeat of what had originally taken place as a result of the broadcast.

The Mercury Theatre received nearly 1,500 letters about the show from listeners. Over 90 per cent of them said they had enjoyed it and it had brightened up an otherwise dull Sunday evening. Others requested more 'realistic' programmes along the same lines.

The show had made the Mercury Theatre the best-known acting company in the United States and the radio series enhanced its reputation outside of New York. It had also brought the organisation a high degree of infamy and a reputation for being, as we would have it today, 'cutting edge' and 'trailblazing'.

But the row had made every network in the United States jittery and many went out of their way to explain to listeners that what they were hearing was either true or false, fact or fiction, 'live' or a recording – causing many humorists and cartoonists to send up the whole concept of censorship. A few days after *The War of the Worlds* was transmitted, radio entertainer Fred Allen planned to include a humorous commentary on his weekly NBC show *Town Hall Tonight* concerning the Martian scare and public reaction to it. His script contained the following:

In view of the recent happenings in radio, I think it would be better, before we start, if I made a sort of announcement: Ladies and Gentlemen, before this radio presentation starts, I would like to announce that this is a comedy programme. Any dialogue or sound effects heard during the next hour will be purely imaginary and will have no relation to any living sounds. If you hear a phone ringing, like this – [telephone rings] – do not pick up your receiver. If you hear a knock, like this – [door knock] – do not run to open your door. Ignore everything you hear on this programme. Just sit back and relax. Nothing is going to happen. And to prove that the offering is positively crammed with nothing, we plunge instantly into the latest news of the week...

Fred Allen never got to deliver his disclaimer. The NBC programme editor insisted on cutting the sequence, fearing that *The War of the Worlds* nerves were still too raw to take any chances, even when disguised as humour.

\* \* \*

As well as infamy, *The War of the Worlds* brought something else to Welles and the Mercury Theatre. Following transmission of the following week's programme, the eighteenth in the series and a tame double-bill of *Heart of Darkness* and *Life with Father*, record audiences tuned in hoping to be scared to death all over again. Towards the end of the show announcer Dan Seymour told the audience, 'In just a moment Orson Welles will return to the microphone with an announcement regarding his future plans.'

As Seymour began reading out cast credits for that evening's programme, audiences across the land began wondering what Welles would tell them. Had he been fired as a result of the previous week's play? Was he to be banned from the airwaves? Was this to be a goodbye to his loyal listeners? Were listeners about to be asked to accept an apology for all the trouble last week's show had caused? Was Orson Welles about to grovel before the American public?

In a grave voice, Welles told the nation:

Ladies and gentlemen, I'm happy at this time to announce that starting Friday 9 December from 9–10 p.m. and each Friday thereafter, we at the Mercury Theatre will be sponsored over most of these stations by the makers of Campbell's Soups. Good night.

Knowing that *The Mercury Theatre on the Air* did not have a commercial sponsor, the soup company's advertising agency had contacted CBS the morning after the famous broadcast expressing interest in sponsoring the show, hoping that no other organisation had beaten them to it. Suddenly CBS threw all thoughts of scrapping the programme out of the window and packed Welles and Houseman off to the soup company's headquarters in Camden, New Jersey (not far from Grover's Mill). They wore their best suits for a tour of the soup factory followed by lunch in the executive dining room – starting with soup – and a formal meeting in the boardroom.

It was agreed that name of the weekly programme would change from *The Mercury Theatre on the Air* to *The Campbell Playhouse*. Welles was not keen on the idea, but knew that sponsorship was worth big money – somewhere between $1,000 and $1,500 every week, and twice that sum to the network in sponsorship revenue.

At the time, Houseman said: 'I guess the soup company figured that if we could sell the end of the world, we could sell tomato soup, too.'

He also recalled:

But there were disadvantages. It soon became apparent that, in some respects, life with Campbell's Soups was going to be less agreeable than when we were our own masters. Previously our only worries had been over the quality of the broadcast and the problems of getting it on the air; now we were concerned with 'format' and with adjusting to the commercials that riddled the broadcast. Welles, in addition to being 'producer, writer, director, star and narrator', now became its leading salesman: he assumed the role of a sophisticated traveller who, having savoured all the greatest broths and potages of the civilised world, still returned with joy and appreciation to Campbell's delicious chicken-and-rice, tomato and pea.

The soup company's advertising agency also felt that Welles and co. should enliven the programme's flavour with more popular fiction. Houseman and Paul Stewart were encouraged to open negotiations for radio rights to the current bestsellers. This was also true of the casting. 'Gone were the happy days of our tight little stock company,' recalled Houseman. 'Each week, after endless bickering with agents and studios, one or more greater or lesser movie stars were brought in to brighten the show.' Mercury actors would in future appear in supporting parts.

The actors recruited would mainly be movie stars, either appearing on Broadway or passing through New York on their way to somewhere else. There were starring roles for Margaret Sullivan, Laurence Olivier, Gertrude Lawrence, Lionel Barrymore, William Powell, Lucille Ball and Jack Benny.

By moving the show from Sundays to a later Friday evening slot, the network would no longer be competing with *The Chase and Sanborn Hour*, allowing the producers to move away from the cosy 'family' feel of the original series and present something more adult, designed to go on air once children had gone to bed. Hence the production of more sophisticated pieces, such as *Rebecca*, *Beau Geste*, *Private Lives*, *What Every Woman Knows* and over forty other 'soupy' programmes between December 1938 and March 1940.

\* \* \*

In the middle of the madness, Welles and Houseman were still attempting to get their much-anticipated production of *Danton's Death* on at their theatre. The opening night had been pushed back several times while Welles defended his decision to annihilate America to the press and caught up on hours of lost sleep sacrificed to rehearsals, which ran into the early hours. Actors playing smaller roles in Mercury stage productions had also threatened to go on strike, claiming that the Actors' Equity rate for their work was $15 a week and not the $10 they were receiving in their pay packets. Other actors – classed as 'supernumeraries' as they had no lines and played in crowd scenes – demanded extra payments of $1 each, claiming that they provided specific cues and 'other business' essential to the play. Thanks to their trade union, all the actors received satisfaction and had their money back-paid, simply because the Mercury Theatre could no longer afford to push the opening night back again and thereby keep paying audiences away.

The curtain finally rose on *Danton's Death* at the Mercury Theatre on the evening of 2 November 1938 and 'house full' notices were positioned in the foyer. While not exactly preparing for Martian monsters triggering death rays across the stage, audience expectation was high.

Brooks Atkinson of *The New York Times* prefaced his review with the following observation:

> Having recovered from frightening the nation over the radio, Orson Welles is now turning his attention to frightening an audience inside the Mercury Theatre. He is doing it deliberately this time in a tingling revival of *Danton's Death*, which finally opened last evening. Since Mr Welles is an erratic genius inside the theatre, the result is overwhelming and a worthy successor to *Caesar* and *Shoemaker's Holiday* of last year.

Atkinson remembered that eleven years previously, Max Reinhardt had produced Büchner's saga of the French Revolution in New York and while the Mercury Theatre's version was 'minute in comparison, Mr Welles manages to give it an impression of spaciousness by putting every inch of the stage to dramatic use'.

The cast – some of whom had taken roles in *The War of the Worlds* – won praise from the critic. Welles, in the part of St Just, played 'in a booming voice with some of the melodramatic solemnity of the Shadow'. He said the production was 'further proof of his [Welles'] power and endows the Mercury Theatre with the same vitality it had last season'.

The review ended on a humorous note:

> Ladies and gentleman, you have just been reading a review of a performance of *Danton's Death* at the Mercury Theatre last evening. It is a play of imagination based on history. There is no occasion for alarm.

Other critics were not so kind and by the end of the first week, audiences were so poor that at least ten Martian death machines could have fitted inside the Mercury Theatre auditorium. The organisation was in deep trouble. Publicity for Orson Welles and the Mercury Theatre had done little or nothing at all for the *Danton's Death* box office receipts. Over half of all bookings were cancelled and the Mercury's usual semi-intellectual, left-wing, lower-middle class audiences were conspicuous by their absence. After twenty-one performances, Welles and Houseman decided to throw in the sponge – not just for *Danton's Death* but also for the Mercury Theatre. They were broke – not just financially, but in spirit, too. Houseman remembered:

In the grandiose and reckless scheme of our lives, the Mercury had fulfilled its purpose. It had brought us success and fame; it had put Welles on the cover of *Time* magazine and our radio show on the front page of every newspaper in the country. Inevitably, any day now, the offers from Hollywood would start arriving. It was too late to turn back – and we did not really want to.

Following the Mercury Theatre's first – and only – theatrical flop, the curtain was rung down for the last time and its actors and technicians were paid off. While the radio show continued and success under the banner of its new sponsor generated larger weekly audiences, things looked decidedly grim for those not taking part in Campbell's Playhouse. They thought they were going to continue working for America's greatest theatre company and had given everything to Welles, working day and night to get his shows onstage, sometimes to the point of nervous breakdowns. They had put up with his tantrums, impatience and a multitude of other shortcomings. And now, with Christmas 1938 just around the corner, they were thrown out of work.

\* \* \*

Just over a week after *The War of the Worlds* went on air, the European political situation worsened. In Germany and Austria on 9–10 November, there was a coordinated attack on Jewish people and their property, which became known as *Kristallnacht*, or the Night of Broken Glass. Over ninety Jews were killed and around 30,000 were arrested and placed in concentration camps. Hundreds of *synagogues* were destroyed and thousands of homes and businesses were ransacked by the Hitler Youth, the Gestapo and the SS.

Early the following year, Germany marched into Bohemia and Moravia, the swastika flew over Slovakia, and Hitler and Mussolini signed their 'Pact of Steel'. On 1 September 1939, Germany invaded Poland and two days later Britain was at war with Germany.

Americans knew it was just a matter of time before they, too, would become involved with the conflict developing on the other side of the ocean. Meanwhile, in April 1939, the New York World's Fair opened its gates, giving the public a chance to relax and enjoy itself by marvelling at pavilions from around the world (Germany stayed away). It offered a glimpse of the great future that lay in store for their country – a land of new prosperity and peace.

The American people would have a long wait…

CHAPTER THIRTEEN

# A Study in Terror

*'Mr Howard K. did not do the actual writing of the* War of the Worlds *script.*
*He only did some of it.'*
—*Letter from Orson Welles to Handley Cantril, 1940*

The American radio-listening and newspaper-reading public finally calmed down two weeks after the broadcast. But people still spoke about it and remembered the impact it had on their families, friends, neighbours and communities.

In the first week of November 1938, Hadley Cantril, a young social psychologist who had established the Office of Public Opinion Research at Princeton University, decided to conduct a research project into American reactions to the broadcast. This became known as the Princeton Radio Project, and was funded by the Rockefeller Foundation with the objective of looking into the effects of mass media on American society. The research was never going to be conclusive, but it was intended to be scientific.

Cantril and his small team planned to conduct personal interviews with 135 different people, over a hundred of whom admitted to having been disturbed by the broadcast. The research was conducted with the full knowledge and co-operation of Welles, Houseman, Koch, the Mercury Theatre and CBS, who were all keen to learn what might be discovered by the exercise.

Cantril estimated that around 6 million people had tuned into the programme at some time on the evening of 30 October, and that 1 million had run to the exits or were or disturbed by it in some way. For reasons of finance and a lack of qualified personnel, interviews were limited to the New Jersey area – the state in which the Martians had landed. Names of respondents were changed to avoid any embarrassment in the event of the survey ever coming into the public domain (which it did in 1940). Interviews began one week after the broadcast and the survey was completed in three weeks.

Mrs Ferguson, a northern New Jersey housewife, was among the interviewees:

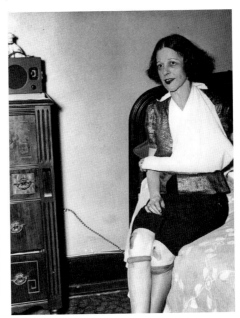

Caroline Cantlon, a WPA actress, was so disturbed by the news of 'smoke in Times Square' that she broke her arm and scraped her knees while fleeing her New York City home. (*AP Newsfeatures*)

I knew it was something terrible and I was frightened, but I didn't know just what it was. I couldn't make myself believe it was the end of the world. I've always heard that when the world comes to an end, it would come so fast nobody would know – so why should God get in touch with this announcer? When they told us what road to take and get up over the hills and the children began to cry, the family decided to go out. We took blankets and my granddaughter wanted to take the cat and the canary. We were outside the garage when the neighbour's boy came back and told us it was a play.

From another small town came Joseph Hendley's report:

That Halloween boo sure had our family on its knees before the programme was half over. God knows but we prayed to Him last Sunday. It was a lesson in more than one thing to us. My mother went out and looked for Mars. Dad was hard to convince or skeptical or sumpin', but he got to believing it. Brother Joe, as usual, got more excited than he could show. Aunt Grace, a good Catholic, began to pray with Uncle Henry. Lily got sick to her stomach. I don't know what I did exactly but I know I prayed harder and more earnestly than ever before. Just as soon as we were convinced that this thing was real, how pretty all things on earth seemed; how soon we put our trust in God.

Archie Burbank, a Newark filling station operator, heard the broadcast while driving his car with a girlfriend. He said:

My girlfriend and I stayed in the car for a while, just driving around. Then we followed the lead of a friend. All of us ran into a grocery store and asked the man if we could go into his cellar. He said, 'What's the matter? Are you trying to ruin my business?' So he chased us out.

A crowd collected. We rushed to an apartment house and asked the man in the apartment to let us in his cellar. He said, 'I don't have a cellar! Get away!'

Then people started to rush out of the apartment house all undressed. We got into the car and listened some more. Suddenly the announcer was gassed, the station went dead so we tried another station but nothing would come on. Then we went to a gas station and filled up our tank in preparation for just riding as far as we could. The gas station man didn't know anything about it. Then one friend, male, decided he would call up the *Newark Evening News*. He found out it was a play. We listened to the rest of the play and then we went dancing.

Sylvia Holmes, a terrified Newark housewife, thinking the end of the world was near, overstepped the bounds of her usual frugality when she heard that aliens had landed in New Jersey:

I found my nephew had come home and gone to bed. I woke him up. I looked in the ice box and saw some chicken left from Sunday dinner. I said to my nephew, 'We may as well eat this chicken – we won't be here in the morning.'

And so the stories went on and Cantril's researchers carefully noted them down word for word for their report. One of the questions asked was, 'At the time you were listening, did you think this broadcast was a play or a real news report?' 28 per cent of those questioned indicated that they believed the broadcast was a news bulletin. 70 per cent of those admitted to being scared in some way. Cantril therefore calculated that around 1.7 million heard the broadcast as a news bulletin and 1.2 million became disturbed by it in some way.

According to Cantril, until *The War of the Worlds*, radio had become the accepted method of hearing important announcements of local, national and international significance, which were often repeated at regular intervals. It must also be remembered that shortly before Welles frightened the bejesus out of so many people, millions of listeners had kept their radios tuned for the latest news from Europe, thought by many to be ready to go to war with America lending support to Britain. They had also begun to become used to programmes being interrupted whenever a serious story broke. All of this helped make *The War of the Worlds* appear real.

New Jersey and Manhattan residents were particularly frightened when they heard mentioned the names of places they knew so well and close to where they were relaxing next to their radio sets. Grover's Mill, Princeton, Trenton, Plainsboro, Allentown, Morristown, the Watchung Mountains, Bayonne, the Hutchinson River Parkway, Newark, the Palisades, Times Square, Fifth Avenue, the Pulaski Skyway and the Holland Tunnel were all familiar to Jerseyites, Philadelphians and New Yorkers. Listeners elsewhere across the United States also recognised many of these names as real places.

Two years after Cantril's study was produced for restricted circulation among broadcasters and academics, the young social psychologist thought that the rest of the country might also be interested in the Princeton Project's findings. Cantril wrote to Welles – who had by now relocated to Hollywood and was attempting to get various film projects off the ground – and informed him of his intention to publish his study in book form and asking if he might endorse Howard Koch's original script, which he planned to reproduce in full. Welles responded that the script was entirely his own. He claimed full authorship of the piece and said that Koch had very little to do with it. He maintained that the idea for the dramatisation was his (which is probably true) and that Koch 'had been helpful' in the second half of the script and 'assisted only a little' on the first part.

Cantril responded that he understood Howard Koch was the sole author and would, as a result, be given full credit when the study was published under the title *The Invasion from Mars*. Welles fired back that any reference to the broadcast script as a dramatisation by Howard Koch was 'something worse than merely untrue'. He said that every one of his collaborators, including members of the cast, had brought more to the script than Koch had.

Welles told Cantril, 'I do strongly feel that you have unwittingly implied a slur on my position as the creator and responsible artist of my broadcasts.'

Cantril fired back with another suggestion. 'Script ideas and development by Orson Welles assisted by John Houseman and Mercury Theatre staff and written by Howard Koch under the direction of Mr Welles.'

Welles was still unhappy and told Cantril that his suggested revision was 'far too elaborate and incorrect a statement. I repeat, *The War of the Worlds* was not written by Howard Koch ... Any statement to this effect is untrue and immeasurably detrimental to me.'

The ball was back in Cantril's court and this time he enclosed copies of affidavits and a telegram from Houseman's secretary stating that Koch had dictated the script to her using a manuscript written by his own hand. It added that Houseman and Paul Stewart had made only minor corrections. Cantril told Welles that, armed with this information, he had no alternative than to acknowledge Koch as writer, although not creator.

Incandescent with rage, Welles stated that surely his word as producer, director and star of the play should hold more weight than the word of one of the authors employed by him at the time. He said that he failed to understand why Cantril had refused to believe he was the sole author: 'Mr Howard K. did not do the actual writing of the *War of the Worlds* script. He only did some of it.' He added that his interest in the matter was not to receive credit for the script, 'but in accuracy'. He asked if Cantril appreciated 'the untold damage done to my professional reputation that the publication of this book in its present form will create. I know that you will understand that I cannot permit this to occur.'

Simon Callow, in *The Road to Xanadu*, the first volume of his biography of Orson Welles, notes that by 1940, none of Welles' Hollywood projects had materialised:

> *The War of the Worlds* was, in effect, his only real claim to widespread fame: it was the reason that he was in Hollywood at all ... the only living proof of his multi-faceted genius. The revelation that he had not actually written it would deprive his image of one of its crucial dimensions, making him look a fraud; the discovery that the whole thing had been an accident would have finished him off for good. Or so it seemed from his pardonably paranoid position.

Callow reveals that Welles lost the battle. Cantril's book, *The Invasion from Mars*, duly appeared with Howard Koch credited as sole author of the script. He writes, 'In the event, no one except Welles even noticed; the legend was undented. The level of his anxiety about all this, however, is a good index of quite how vulnerable he felt in April 1940.'

Cantril's book, produced by an academic publisher, is still in print today and available to anyone interested in the science of communications, mass behavior and the effect a Sunday evening radio play had on American public life over seventy years ago.

# CHAPTER FOURTEEN

# Mr Welles Meets Mr Wells

*'The crisis of today is the joke of tomorrow.'*
*—H. G. Wells*

H. G. Wells was no stranger to the world of cinema and entertainment. By 1940, at least twelve of his stories had been turned into silent or talking pictures, starting in 1919 with a screen treatment of *The First Men in the Moon*.

Wells loved everything about movies and moviemaking. He liked the company of film directors and producers, screenwriters and pretty actresses. In 1936, a film version of his 1933 novel *The Shape of Things to Come* went before the cameras at Alexander Korda's London Films studios at Denham in Buckinghamshire. Wells had written a screenplay from his own book and Korda had gathered together a strong cast including Raymond Massey, Ralph Richardson and Cedric Hardwick. His oldest son, Frank Wells, was engaged as an assistant art director.

In addition to screenwriting duties, Korda also gave Wells artistic control over the project, and the author took advantage of his freedom, firing at least one leading actor and replacing him with another more to his liking. He personally supervised nearly every aspect of the film, including casting, art direction and the music, composed by Arthur Bliss. He even had a hand in designing posters for the film, which became known to filmgoers as *H. G. Wells' Things to Come* – with the words 'an Alexander Korda production' appearing in smaller type.

Wells came to the set on most days and loved to sit on the sidelines to watch director William Cameron Menzies and his technicians and actors at work. By the time Wells visited the USA in 1940, he had a pretty good idea of who was who in the Hollywood film colony.

In October of that year, Wells was in America promoting his forthcoming novel, *Babes in the Darkling Wood*, and delivering lectures to institutions and associations with enough money to pay his high fees. He was also hoping to meet American film producers interested in turning his stories into Hollywood pictures.

H. G. Wells arrived in the United States in 1940. 'The best thing that happened was meeting my little namesake, Orson. I find him the most delightful fellow.' (*Library of Congress*)

On 28 October, he found himself in San Antonio, Texas, where he had been engaged by the United States Brewers' Association to deliver an address on trade relations between Britain and the United States. Another well-known figure whose words famously resonated with the public was also in town, as part of a lecture tour of American cities. His name was Orson Welles.

Welles was taking a break from Hollywood, where he had finished overseeing principal photography of his first film, *Citizen Kane*, featuring actors from the Mercury Theatre. About six weeks' work on the film was still left, but RKO refused to pay Welles any more money until he handed over the completed picture. As usual, Welles needed cash and closed film production for two weeks to go on the road and give public lectures while Hollywood post-production work continued in his absence.

It is not known who informed either of the men that the other was in town, but someone somehow managed to bring them together on the evening that both arrived in Texas' second-largest city.

In all probability, twenty-six-year-old Orson Welles had a speech of apology ready for Mr Wells two years after his free adaptation of the other man's *The*

*War of the Worlds* had created nationwide mayhem. Seventy-four-year-old H. G. Wells was probably ready to thank his younger namesake for boosting sales of his novel, which was quickly rushed back into print by Grosset & Dunlap with a cover reproducing the screaming headlines published after the broadcast, and the tagline, 'The book that terrified the nation over the air!' For the second time in its publishing life, *The War of the Worlds* became a bestseller, although many American readers were disappointed when they opened the book to discover that Martians had not landed at Grover's Mill, New Jersey, but somewhere called Horsell Common in Surrey, England.

The two men met informally and got along like a house on fire. By 1940, H. G. Wells had mellowed and all talk of legal action with the younger Welles was long-forgotten. They spoke about filmmaking, setting up a meeting with Cecil B. de Mille and the possibility of turning *The War of the Worlds* into a film with a script by H. G. Wells to be directed – of course – by Orson. They discussed literature, the state of the world, and politics. The older Wells found the younger Welles charming, polite and terrific company. H. G. Wells was so impressed with the 'young genius' that the pair agreed to give a short interview to the local San Antonio radio station the following day.

Bagging two of the most famous personalities from the world of entertainment and literature at the same time – and in San Antonio of all places – was a real coup for Radio KTSA and its interviewer, Charles C. Shaw. The interview was warm and relaxed with plenty of laughter in the studio once the pair arrived ready to take their places behind the microphone.

\* \* \*

Shaw commences proceedings with a long, respectful, ingratiating and flattering introduction to Mr Welles and Mr Wells:

SHAW: Good evening ladies and gentlemen, this is Charles C. Shaw speaking; KTSA is honoured this evening by the presence in our studio of two great men – the honourable H. G. Wells, world famous British historian and student of world affairs, and Mr Orson Welles, the genius of stage, screen and radio. This is the first time that Mr H. G. Wells and Mr Orson Welles have appeared together. In fact they only met for the first time yesterday here in San Antonio, but this is not the first time their names have been linked. Two years ago Mr Orson Welles adapted Mr H. G. Wells' book *The War of the Worlds* for radio purposes. You know the rest. Revising the story somewhat, Mr Orson Welles depicted an invasion of the United States by men from Mars. Although he explained numerous times in the programme that it was fictitious, the country was frightened almost out of its wits. Men called radio stations offering to enlist against the Martians, others were panic-stricken. The realism of the production, frightening though it was, is a fantastic tribute to Mr Orson Welles' genius. And thus, the names of Mr Orson Welles and Mr H. G. Wells became linked. Mr H. G. Wells, in the opinion of many, is the world's most famous man of letters. He has come to San Antonio to address the United States Brewers' Association and Mr Orson Welles is here for a town hall formal address on Wednesday. In this meeting of great minds I feel inconspicuous, and the less I have to say the better you listeners will like it. But first, can I interest you gentlemen in a discussion of Mr Orson Welles' broadcast of the Mr H. G. Wells' book *The War of the Worlds*?

There is a pause and neither guest is certain who is to speak first. Orson Welles is first to break the silence:

ORSON WELLES: Are you turning the meeting over to us, sir?

SHAW: I am at the moment.

H. G. WELLS: He's turning it over to us! Well, I've had a series of the most delightful experiences since I came to America. But the best thing that has happened so far, is meeting my little namesake here, Orson. I find him the

On 29 October 1940, Welles met Wells while they were both in San Antonio, Texas. Together they took part in a special radio programme – and got along like a house on fire. (*Author's collection*)

most delightful carrier. He carries my name with an extra 'e', which I hope he will drop sooner or later. [Laughter from Welles.] I see no sense in it. I've known his work before he made this sensational Halloween spree. Are you sure there was such a panic in America – or was it just your Halloween fun?

ORSON WELLES: I think that's the nicest thing that a man from England could possibly say about the men from Mars. Mr Hitler made a good deal of sport over it, you know. He actually spoke of it in the great Munich speech and there were floats and Nazi propaganda afterwards...

H. G. WELLS: That's because he didn't have much to say...

There is more laughter in the studio. Then:

ORSON WELLES: And it's supposed to show the corrupt condition and decadence and state of affairs in democracies that *The War of the Worlds* went over as it did. I think it's very nice of Mr Wells to say that not only I didn't mean it, but the American people didn't mean it.

H. G. WELLS: That's our impression in England. We read articles about it and people said, 'Have you never heard of Halloween in American where everybody tends to see ghosts?' [Orson Welles laughs.] Now before we get away from this microphone, tell me about this film of yours which you're producing. You're a producer, aren't you? And art director? You're everything. What's the film called?

ORSON WELLES: It's called *Citizen Kane*.

H. G. WELLS: Citizen Kane? Not C-A-I-N-E?

ORSON WELLES: No, K-A-N-E. And this is the kindest and most gracious thing it's possible to do; Mr Wells is making it possible for me to do what in America is spoken of as a 'plug'.

H. G. WELLS: I don't always understand these words...

ORSON WELLES: But you understand their value. Mr Wells wants me to tell you that I've made a motion picture and he's kind enough to ask me a leading question concerning it...

H. G. WELLS: I'm looking forward to it.

ORSON WELLES: You're very kind, sir. It's a new sort of picture with a new method of presentation and a few new technical experiments and a few new methods of telling a picture, not just from the point of view of writing, but of showing it…

H. G. WELLS: If I don't misunderstand you completely, there'll be a lot of jolly good new noises in it…

Laughter in the studio.

ORSON WELLES: I hope so. A lot of jolly good new noises. It's something that motion pictures could well afford these days. I hope you're right and that there are some jolly good new noises. I can think of nothing more desirable in a motion picture. I'm all for jolly good new noises…

There follows some general talk about the use – and non-use of scenery in the theatre and H. G. Wells uses the occasion to put in a plug for his forthcoming novel *Babes in the Darkling Wood*, which would be published in America the following year. Orson Welles appears to have already read it and says it is a very good book, for which H. G. Wells thanks him:

H. G. WELLS: I think that for a man I've only met for two days, Orson's a very loyal cousin of mine.

After just seven minutes, Shaw has to wrap up the interview 'with great reluctance.' He says that the interview 'has been one of the real pleasures of my life'. He thanks Mr Wells and Mr Welles 'for honouring us with your presence tonight. Our heartfelt thanks for your kindness.'

\* \* \*

Messrs Welles and Wells went their separate ways. H. G. returned to England to complete work on his next book, *You Can't Be Too Careful*, a novel met by critical indifference during the early years of the Second World War, and Orson returned to Hollywood to complete *Citizen Kane*, a box office disaster that was hailed a masterpiece when it began appearing on television in the 1950s. It is now considered one of the greatest films of all time.

# Not-so-Happy Endings

*'If you want a happy ending, it depends, of course, where you stop your story.'*
—*Orson Welles*

Throughout the rest of his life, Welles was often asked to reflect on the impact *The War of the Worlds* had on the American nation. Seventeen years after the programme, Welles spoke about this in a 1955 series for the BBC called *Orson Welles' Sketchbook*:

> I suppose we had it coming to us, because in fact we weren't as innocent as we were meant to be when we did the Martian broadcast. We were fed up with the way in which everything that came over this new magic box, the radio, was being swallowed. People, you know, do suspect what they read in the newspapers and what people tell them, but when the radio came – and I suppose now television – anything that came through that new machine was believed. So in a way our broadcast was an assault on the credibility of that machine; we wanted people to understand that they shouldn't take any opinion pre-digested and they shouldn't swallow everything that came through the tap, whether it was radio or not. But … it was only a partial experiment; we had no idea the extent of the thing and I certainly personally had no idea what it would mean to me.

In his 1992 book *This Is Orson Welles*, which was based on recorded conversations with Welles, author and film director Peter Bogdanovich managed to extract an extraordinary confession from Welles by asking if he had any idea of the response the show would generate. Welles replied: 'The *kind* of response was merrily anticipated by us all. The *size*, of course, was flabbergasting.'

Talking to Leslie Megahey in 1982 for his two-part documentary *The Orson Welles Story*, Welles said that the *War of the Worlds* idea came about 'because we had a lot of real radio nuts on as commentators at this period. People who wanted to keep us out of European entanglements and a fascist priest called

Father Coughlin, and people believed anything they heard on the radio. And I said: "Let's do something impossible and make them believe it. And then tell them, show them, that it's only radio." So that was what started it ... And I got a contact to Hollywood; it really is the truth.'

Speaking on *The Dean Martin Show* in 1970, when he was a regular guest usually given to delivering a monologue, a poem or a piece from Shakespeare, Welles said that there used to be a time when every second person who caught sight of him in the street used to enquire, 'How's the man from Mars?'

But time is a great healer. Welles added:

Today there are millions of people who don't even know what happened that Halloween night on the radio. Back then, radio was really big. It was also a big piece of furniture in our living rooms, like TV is today, and it occupied a big piece of our lives. It was also a voice of authority; too much so – at least I thought so. I figured it was time to take the Mickey out of some of that authority. Hence my broadcast of *The War of the Worlds* ... This was on Halloween, remember, and in my Midwestern childhood, this was the season for pranks and spooking the neighbours with a pumpkin head. Well, in that notorious broadcast I said 'boo' to several million people over a full network and the pumpkin was a flying saucer from Mars. Trouble was that an awful lot of listeners forgot what day it was.

\* \* \*

The world had to wait until 1950 before the Martians tried to get their own back on Orson Welles – and it was all thanks to the 'Man of Steel' himself... Superman!

By 1949 Welles had left Hollywood for Europe to appear in *Black Magic*, a film adaptation of the Alexandre Dumas novel *Joseph Balsamo*. The end credits state that the film was directed by Gregory Ratoff, but Welles is understood to have directed most of the sequences. The film is a swirling and swashbuckling romantic drama in which Welles plays eighteenth-century hypnotist and magician Balsamo, a.k.a. Count Cagliostro.

As a special 'tie-in' promotion for the film's 1950 American release, United Artists came to an arrangement with the world's largest publishers of comic books, DC Comics, to produce an edition featuring both Superman and Orson Welles together in a sci-fi adventure story called *Black Magic on Mars*.

Underneath the Superman cover logo, readers learned that the issue featured 'Orson Welles, star of *Black Magic* in an astounding adventure with The Man of Steel! The man who startled America does it again...!'

The cover showed typical comic book Martians, with lightbulb-shaped heads, pointing ray guns at Superman, who is seen catching the deathly rays

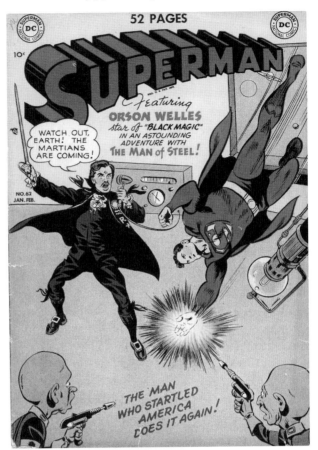

'Watch out Earth! The Martians are coming!' yells 'the man who startled America' to the Man of Steel in the 1950s comic-book adventure 'Black Magic on Mars'. (*SUPERMAN*™ *and © DC Comics. All rights reserved.*)

with his bare hands. Welles holds a microphone to his lips and yells, 'Watch out Earth! The Martians are coming!'

The story opens with Welles, wearing the magician's costume from the film, engaged in a duel over the rooftops of an eighteenth-century town. Suddenly Welles slips and plummets to the cobbled street below. A voice cries 'Cut!' and readers learn that the duel was part of a movie being shot on location. The director tells the cast that there will be a fancy dress party that evening and everyone must arrive wearing the costume they wore in the scene shot that day.

Later Welles (who could not drive) is pictured driving up a mountain highway, where he comes across a space rocket at the side of the road. In a speech bubble he thinks, 'This baby looks powerful enough to reach another planet.' A door in the side of the rocket is conveniently open and Welles enters just as an announcement is heard saying that the door is closing 'and shortly the first pilotless rocket will be blasting off for Mars'.

It is too late for Welles to climb out, 'and as the rocket ship plunges into the black abyss of outer space, Orson Welles takes a last look at his own planet!'

In a speech bubble, Welles thinks to himself, 'When I fooled the world with my Martian invasion broadcast, I never dreamed that *I* would invade Mars myself.'

Two hours later the rocket lands on Mars and the door opens, allowing Welles 'to step out into the soil of another world'. Seconds later he meets a little grey alien wearing a Nazi-style uniform. 'Hail Welles,' says the alien. 'We have come to take you before our master, the Great Martler.'

Welles observes, 'They speak English and look like Nazis – and Martler sounds like Hitler!'

The chief Martler, who does indeed bear an uncanny alien resemblance to a certain dead European dictator, tells Welles, 'I admired your Hitler and I will Blitzkrieg the Solar System, starting with Earth.'

A speech bubble tells readers what Welles is thinking: 'If only I could warn Earth.'

Producing the sword he has been using in the film (and is still conveniently wearing), Welles yells at the Martian chief: 'You're nothing but an old-fashioned dictator. Get back or I'll run you through.'

At sword point, Welles leads Martler into the Martian broadcasting studio and orders him to demonstrate how to send a message back to Earth. Martler complies.

Welles speaks into the microphone: 'Attention Superman! This is Orson Welles broadcasting from Mars. I have no time to tell you how I came to be here. I have time only to warn you that the Martians are coming with a fleet of rocket ships to invade Earth – and they will be there within hours.'

But Earthlings laugh at the warning. For them, this is the second time that Orson Welles has cried wolf. In the office of the *Daily Planet* newspaper, editor Perry White and reporter Clark Kent are tuned into the radio. Welles' voice is heard: 'You must believe me. The Martians really are coming! At this very moment they are threatening me with ray guns... Help Superman!'

The newspaper editor says it's another Welles hoax and who does he think he's kidding? But Clark Kent knows otherwise: 'My telescopic vision tells me that this is a job for Superman!' Soon he is flying faster than the speed of light through space to rescue Welles, capture Martler with a biff, bang, boff, and dump him onto a remote asteroid where he will be out of trouble.

The comic book concludes: 'With transportation provided by Superman, Orson is in time for the costume ball that evening. The entire adventure has taken less than eight hours since completion at noon of the filming of *Black Magic*.'

Welles is seen at the ball dancing closely to his beautiful female co-star, who asks, 'Tell me Orson, was your broadcast this time another hoax... or the truth?'

Welles replies: 'Ask Superman!'

Welles never mentioned the comic book in any interviews. He must have given permission for his name and image to be used (although none of the drawings looked remotely like Orson Welles) and DC Comics might even have paid him a fee. The *Black Magic on Mars* comic book is now a collector's item, selling for over £130 on specialist websites.

*  *  *

The Hollywood film community was not best pleased when Welles arrived in their midst in 1939. Those who had worked their way up from bit parts to become fully fledged movie stars and the assistant props men who were now movie directors resented the arrival of New York's twenty-four-year-old boy genius, who had total artistic control as producer, writer, director and star. They also envied his $100,000-a-year salary, which was more than that earned by President Roosevelt.

The RKO film studio bankrolled Welles and gave him total freedom to develop his own stories, use his own cast and crew and have final cut privilege – something no one else had ever been given before and few have been given since. Various projects were considered for his first film and much preparation went into producing a screen version of Conrad's *Heart of Darkness*, which was later scrapped. It was during this period that Welles was quoted as saying that working in the film industry was like owning 'the biggest electric train set a boy ever had!'

As the world knows, his first film was the iconic *Citizen Kane*, which he directed, co-wrote and starred in, alongside actors from the Mercury Theatre. When rumour got out that the film's central character, newspaper tycoon Charles Foster Kane, was a thinly disguised version of American media baron William Randolph Hearst, attempts were made to ban the film and have all prints destroyed. Hearst owned more newspapers than any other media giant in the United States and on instructions from the man himself, no mention of *Citizen Kane* was made in any of them – ever.

RKO got cold feet. Although *Citizen Kane* was met with respectful reviews elsewhere, it soon disappeared from view. By this time Welles was engaged on his next film featuring Mercury actors, *The Magnificent Ambersons*. But the story of his fall from Hollywood grace and his ongoing struggles to write, direct and appear in films is told in depth elsewhere.

Welles spent the last fifteen years of his life appearing on talk shows, providing a highly recognisable voice for numerous television commercials, appearing in a steady flow of good and bad films (with the bad far outnumbering the good) and trying to get his own movie projects off the ground. He once reflected, 'I started at the top and worked my way down.'

Welles was always a large man. He had a gargantuan appetite for food as well as life. In later years he became obese and had to be taken everywhere in a wheelchair. His famous appetite became part of his own self-deprecating humour, something rarely evident during his early years but present in later ones when he appeared on talk shows. He often admitted that it 'was not good to be fat'. He would say, 'My doctor told me to stop having intimate dinners for four – unless there are three other people present.'

He won many awards in his lifetime for direction, acting and other contributions to the cinema, including an Academy Award for co-writing the script of *Citizen Kane* with Herman J. Mankiewicz. The film received a total of nine Academy Award nominations and Welles was nominated for Best Actor in a Leading Role. But he did not win that night and the only other Academy Award won by Welles was a 1971 'Honorary Oscar' for 'superlative artistry and versatility in the creation of motion pictures'. It was the very same people who honoured him with this award that refused to give him work and were 'out to lunch' whenever he called.

Welles spent his entire life ploughing his own furrow, but to do this he all too often had to climb on board someone else's inferior tractor to earn a living.

He died on 10 October 1985, aged seventy, following an appearance on Merv Griffin's daytime television talk show. Welles had recently shed a third of his weight. Although his face looked drawn, he was relaxed and mellow as Griffin asked about painful times in his life. Welles admitted, 'There's all kinds of pain. Bad conscious pain – that's the worst. I have regrets. There are times I didn't behave as well as I ought to have. And that's a real pain.'

The final words Welles publicly uttered were in answer to a question about his early radio career. Griffin asked Welles if he saw any connection between modern-day television soap operas and the kind he had produced for *The Mercury Theatre on the Air* and *The Campbell Playhouse*. Welles replied:

> I acted in soap operas to make my living. But my own shows weren't soap operas. We did the same thing you make movies out of, full-length stories with only one commercial break. I was young then. I was awful busy. And awful lucky. I had a tremendous streak of luck and I'm very grateful for that. I'm not being fake modest talking about luck, but I do believe luck has everything to do with anyone's life.

Two hours later, Welles collapsed following a myocardial infarction – a heart attack – at his home near Hollywood Boulevard. He was later found dead hunched over his typewriter, where he had been writing a script called *The Magic Show*. His ashes were buried in an old well covered by flowers, within the rural property of long-time friend and retired bullfighter Antonio Ordóñez in Ronda, Spain, where a street is also named in his honour.

Most of the films Orson Welles made as a director and actor can be found on DVD, although one or two take some hunting down. However, the plays he produced for *The Mercury Theatre on the Air* – including *The War of the Worlds* – are available on CDs or can be heard online. Over seventy years later, the shows hold up remarkably well considering the chaos, temper and tantrums that surrounded each show. In 2001, *Time* magazine paid a special tribute to 'Awesome' Welles and his Sunday evening Mercury shows:

> Don't look at what he was forced to become in the public eye. Listen, in rapture, at the sounds, stories, people and emotions that Welles was able to create, back when he and radio were young, with all that achievement, and all that promise.

\* \* \*

Welles had fallen out with John Houseman a year after arriving in Hollywood. Houseman felt he had been shoved into a corner and no longer served any useful purpose to Welles. He went on to become vice president of David O. Selznick Productions, and following the war with Japan became head of the overseas radio division of the Office of War Information.

After the war he produced nearly twenty films for Paramount, Universal and MGM including the 1946 film noir *The Blue Dahlia*, the 1953 film adaptation of *Julius Caesar* starring Marlon Brando and *Lust for Life* featuring Kirk Douglas as Vincent van Gogh.

But it was as an actor that Houseman became known to the wider cinema-going public when he appeared as the cantankerous Professor Charles Kingsfield in the 1973 film *The Paper Chase*. He only took on the role as a favour to the director, but he ended up receiving an Academy Award for Best Supporting Actor – a prize that had eluded Orson Welles for his entire career. He went on to repeat the role in the television series of the same name in 1978–86, receiving two Golden Globe nominations for 'Best Actor in a TV Series – Drama'.

Houseman died of cancer at the age of eighty-six on Halloween night in 1988, having met Orson Welles on only two further occasions since he and the one-time wunderkind had parted company nearly half a century before. A Broadway theatre is named in his honour. Welles never once mentioned Houseman or acknowledged the huge part he had played in his career in the many interviews he gave to newspapers, magazines, radio and television. Houseman, however, paid full tribute to Welles – the good, bad and ugly – in his autobiography *Unfinished Business*.

Howard Koch went on to have a Hollywood career of his own, writing scripts and collaborating on others for various studios. Koch contributed to the popular film *Casablanca*, starring Humphrey Bogart and Ingrid Bergman, which he co-scripted with Julius and Philip Epstein in 1942 and for which they shared an Academy Award. He also penned *Shining Victory* (1941) and *Letter from an Unknown Woman* (1948). He collaborated on screenplays for *The Sea Hawk* (starring Errol Flynn), *The Letter* (starring Bette Davis) and *Sergeant York* (directed by Howard Hawks and starring Gary Cooper).

In 1943, and at the request of Jack L. Warner of Warner Bros, Koch wrote the screenplay for *Mission to Moscow*, which went on to create controversy because of its positive portrayal of Joseph Stalin and the Soviet Union. Warner later fired Koch after the writer was denounced as a Communist. He went on to be criticised by the House Un-American Activities Committee for his 'outspoken leftist political views' and in 1951 was blacklisted by Hollywood.

Koch fled with his family to England, where he teamed up with other blacklisted writers. For five years he wrote for film and television under various pseudonyms.

By 1956 it was safe to return to the United States. He bought a home in Woodstock, New York, and continued to write plays, scripts, books and articles and remained actively committed to progressive political causes and to social justice.

In 1988 – the fiftieth anniversary year of the broadcast – Howard Koch's original forty-seven-page typewritten script went up for auction at Sotheby's New York auction house. The script was the only one of only two known to exist following the police raid on the CBS studios in October 1938, when all the other copies were confiscated and destroyed. It had been sitting in a filing cabinet at Koch's home for half a century. He told *The New York Times*, 'It was just sitting there and wasn't being seen by anybody. A friend said to me, "If you've got that script, it's very valuable."'

The script was signed by Koch and included annotations by Welles, Houseman and CBS censors. Sotheby's expected fierce bidding for the script and estimated that it might fetch as much as $35,000. In fact, it was sold for $143,000 to an anonymous buyer. 'I had a private offer of $60,000 but was advised to take the gamble. I guess it was the right gamble,' said Koch later.

Howard Koch died in 1995 in Kingston, New York. On his desk, awaiting completion, was a novel. Its title? *Invasion from Mars*.

\* \* \*

In June 1994 Christie's East in New York auctioned a copy of Orson Welles' original director's script. Hollywood's hottest film director, Steven Spielberg, was the winning bidder. A website devoted to Orson Welles, *www.wellesnet.com*, claims that Spielberg bought the script to add to his collection of high-priced Welles memorabilia, 'including, in what Welles considered a delicious irony, a FAKE copy of the Rosebud sled [from *Citizen Kane*], which Spielberg had paid $60,000 to own'.

The final price paid by Spielberg for the Welles script is unknown, but was given a pre-sale estimate by Christie's of $15,000–20,000. Wellesnet takes up the story:

Buying Welles' copy of the script was also Spielberg's impetus for making his own movie version of *War of the Worlds* in 2005. While doing interviews to promote his movie, Spielberg told *Hotdog* magazine: 'If I could have, I would have begun this movie twelve years ago. I had bought at an auction the last surviving *War Of The Worlds* radio script and it was amazing, I guess you could say it was a distillation of the novel. I said, "Oh man, this would make an amazing movie." Then, when *Independence Day* came out I said, "Well, maybe I won't make it," because they kind of picked the bones off that and it put me off for a while. Then I got interested in it again just in the course of trying to find something to do with Tom Cruise.'

This is the Christie's catalogue description of the script:

ORSON WELLES: Typescript radio play *The War of The Worlds* (New York, 1938).

45 pages – (8 x 10 in.) typed on one side only, some pages with original drawings by Welles in heavy pencil of faces and oddly alien creatures. In very fine condition.

Along with a letter written and signed to an unidentified correspondent by Orson Welles. No date, on original printed Mercury Theatre stationery, 8x10 inches.

In the letter Welles writes: 'This is to certify that this is my own directorial copy of *The War of The Worlds* radio script. Needless to say I scarcely anticipated the reaction accorded what seemed to us to be a fairly routine hour radio show. Orson Welles.'

## ORSON WELLES' DIRECTOR'S TYPESCRIPT OF *THE WAR OF THE WORLDS*

Only one other copy is known to exist. On October 30, 1938, Orson Welles and *The Mecury Theatre an the Air* presented what listeners believed was a live performance of Ramon Raquello and his Orchestra. History was made that evening as the fictitious Intercontinental Radio News network interrupted with flash bulletins reporting terrifying, dramatic sightings of the dreaded Aliens from Mars. A nationwide panic ensued and Welles found himself at the center of what is still considered to be the most famous backfired hoax of all time. Numerous injuries due to the panic were reported and CBS and the New York City Police Department confiscated all copies of the script. Until now, writer Howard Koch's copy had been believed to be the only complete typescript in existence. Welles gave this script to a close associate of his for safekeeping.

The forty-five-page script is annotated with drawings by Welles in heavy pencil, most of alien Martian images, according to the text. On the first page is a full page drawing of a robust man, signed in pencil at the bottom, 'Orson Welles'.

* * *

Many others associated with the famous 1938 broadcast went on to have long and varied careers in film, theatre, radio and television.

Unfortunately, Bernard Herrmann – the temperamental maestro who reluctantly conducted 'popular' music for *The War of the Worlds* and scores of other plays presented by *The Mercury Theatre on the Air* – is remembered for his rude and obnoxious behavior towards many he worked with. After leaving his post as chief conductor with the CBS Symphony Orchestra to follow Welles to Hollywood and compose the score for *Citizen Kane*, he rapidly gained a reputation for being 'difficult'. His unfortunate attitude, outspoken remarks and violent temper resulted in many filmmakers refusing to use his talents.

Others, however, recognised his genius and he went on to compose thrilling music for around fifty films, including an Oscar-nominated score for *Citizen Kane* and an Oscar-winning score for *The Devil and Daniel Webster*, plus memorable music for *Psycho*, *North by Northwest*, *Jane Eyre*, *The Man Who Knew Too Much*, *Jason and the Argonauts*, *The Birds* and *Taxi Driver*. Besides his work with Welles, he composed the scores for films made by William Dieterle, Alfred Hitchcock, François Truffaut, Brian De Palma and Martin Scorsese.

In 1973 this most 'difficult' of men was asked to reflect on his relationship with Orson Welles. He remembered:

> People always tell me how difficult Orson Welles is. The only people I've ever met worth working for were difficult people – because they're interested in achieving something. Just spare me the charmers. Welles in every other way might be difficult, but when it comes to making artistic decisions he's like the Rock of Gibraltar.

Bernard Herrmann died in 1965 at the age of sixty-four. Today he is regarded as one of the best composers to have worked in films between the early 1940s and the 1970s. His scores are often featured at concerts of movie music and the screeching violins used in the famous shower scene in Alfred Hitchcock's *Psycho* are even a popular mobile phone ringtone.

By the time *The War of the Worlds* was about to be broadcast to a surprised nation, CBS boss William S. Paley was planning to axe *The Mercury Theatre on the Air*'s weekly series because of disappointing ratings. When Paley and his associates saw reaction to the notorious broadcast in the following day's newspapers, they quickly woke up to the fact that they had a goldmine on their hands and the Campbell Soup Company stepped in to save the show with handsome sponsorship.

Paley was twice married, his first wife being Dorothy Hart Hearst, the former wife of the third son of Citizen Kane himself – William Randolph

Hearst. Paley was a discreet womaniser whose most famous mistress was the silent screen star Louise Brooks, for whom he maintained a stipend that allowed her to live in comfort for the rest of her life. Paley died aged eighty-nine in 1990.

Howard Smith, who played valiant US Army bomber pilot Lieutenant Voght – who sacrifices both himself and his plane by crash-landing on the Martian tripods – began his acting career in silent films before working in radio, film and television. He was a regular performer in *The Twilight Zone* and other series, including *Perry Mason* and *Green Acres*. He died in Hollywood in 1968.

Paul Stewart was a founder member of the Mercury Theatre group, having met Welles in 1934, when he hired the young actor for a role in *The American School of the Air*, a half-hour educational radio series broadcast by CBS on weekday afternoons.

Stewart played one of the radio announcers in *The War of the Worlds*, an appropriate part for Stewart because his voice was familiar to radio listeners and Welles knew that the audience would find him convincing. He began his film career in the early 1940s and portrayed the wily valet Raymond in *Citizen Kane*. His dark looks and deep voice won him dozens of 'sinister type' and 'tough guy' roles in *Champion* (1949), *Twelve O'Clock High* (1949) and *The Man Who Never Was* (1966).

In the 1950s and 1960s Stewart turned to stage and TV, directing shows including *Peter Gunn*, *Perry Mason*, *Hawaii 5-0* and *Remington Steele*. He died following a fatal heart attack in 1986, aged seventy-seven.

The last surviving member of *The War of the Worlds* cast is ninety-four-year-old William Herz, who played 'Radio Operator 8X3R' and the Newark radio operator in the show. He still lives in New York and every week dines at Broadway's famous Sardi's restaurant, where he has been eating since 1933. He enjoys looking back on his career with the Mercury Theatre. Asked what he remembers about Welles, he recalled, 'You had to have a strong, strong stomach, because he was a genius, but he was a difficult man to work with. He only looked about twenty-one, and maybe he might have been twenty-two. He was awfully young, and he was a man who didn't think. He just did!'

William Alland was a regular performer with *The Mercury Theatre on the Air* and played the role of the Meridian Room announcer and a field artillery gunner in *The War of the Worlds*. Welles cast Alland in the important role of investigative reporter Jerry Thompson, sent to find out who – or what – 'Rosebud' is in *Citizen Kane*.

Alland went on to become a radio producer and won a Peabody Award for his true-to-life radio documentary series *Doorway to Life*, about children's psychological problems, aired in 1947/48. He was also a producer and director of Hollywood westerns and science fiction, including *Chief Crazy Horse*, *Tarantula*, *This Island Earth*, *The Mole People* and *It Came From*

A bronze monument in Van Nest Park at the edge of Grover's Mill Pond, New Jersey. (*Author's Collection*)

*Outer Space*. He proudly claimed that all of his films made a profit. He died in California in 1997.

Ray Collins emerged as one of the Mercury Theatre's most successful actors. The son of a newspaper drama critic, he began his theatrical career at the age of fourteen and after years of hard work secured his place at the Mercury Theatre.

In *The War of the Worlds*, Collins portrayed Mr Wilmuth, owner of the farm in Grover's Mill where the Martians land, and the lone reporter who witnesses the destruction of New York City until it is overwhelmed by poisonous black smoke pouring from the alien walking machines. For many years he also played opposite Welles as Police Commissioner Weston on *The Shadow* radio series.

Collins appeared in over ninety films, including *Citizen Kane*, *The Magnificent Ambersons*, *Touch of Evil*, *The Heiress* and *The Best Years of Our Lives*, before taking on the role of the tough, gruff-voiced Lt Tragg on the *Perry Mason* TV series. He died in 1965.

Kenny Delmar, who played the secretary of state in *The War of the Worlds* – and was mistaken for President Franklin D. Roosevelt by many listeners – began acting as a child in silent films, including D. W. Griffith's *Orphans of the Storm*.

He graduated into radio and thanks to his skill at vocal characterisations and quick wit landed a regular part on *The Fred Allen Show* as the brash, blustering Southern Senator Beauregard Claghorn, who delighted audiences with his corny puns. The character was so popular that the Warner Bros cartoon department created a character named Foghorn Leghorn, voiced by Mel Blanc, as a tribute.

Remaining a New York-based actor until his retirement, Delmar spent the 1960s providing voiceovers for TV commercials and cartoon programmes. He died in 1984.

Stefan Schnabel, who played a US Army artillery observer in the *War of the Worlds* sequence in which listeners are taken to the front line of a valiant infantry battle against the Martian walking machines, was the son of classical pianist Artur Schnabel.

Born in Germany, he fled to the United States when the Nazis came to power. Already an experienced actor, he had spent time at London's Old Vic and was a regular player with *The Mercury Theatre on the Air*.

Schnabel worked with Welles on other projects, including a disastrous Broadway musical adaptation of Jules Verne's novel *Around the World in Eighty Days*.

After a long and varied film career, in which he appeared in *Houdini*, *Firefox* and Welles' *Journey into Fear*, Schnabel landed a seventeen-year contract to appear in the long-running daytime television soap opera, *The Guiding Light*. He died in 1999.

Carl Frank, who portrayed the ranting stranger alongside Welles' Professor Pierson, was born in 1909. His early career included regular stints on the radio soap *Buck Rogers in the 25th Century* and various roles on *The Shadow*, where he first met Welles.

Frank also played the radio announcer whose announcement interrupts the phony programme of evening music in *The War of the Worlds*. He moved on to a film and television career and often appeared in television versions of radio classics that he had once performed in front of a microphone. He died in 1972.

*The Mercury Theatre on the Air*'s announcer Dan Seymour was born in 1914. He began his career as a radio announcer in 1935 and the following year he joined the Columbia Broadcasting System in New York, where he used his deep and mellow voice to present numerous shows.

At the time of his death in 1982, Seymour was serving as a director of several companies, including American Express. He had served as president and later chairman of the board of the J. Walter Thompson advertising agency in the 1960s and early 70s.

Frank Readick, who played radio eyewitness reporter Carl Phillips – the first reporter onto the scene at Grover's Mill – was born in 1896. His chilling performance was inspired by listening to a wax disc recording of Herb Morrison reporting the *Hindenburg* disaster.

In 1931, Readick made his main contribution to radio history when he succeeded James La Curto for three years as the voice of crime's dark avenger, *The Shadow* – a part later to be played by Orson Welles.

By the time *The War of the Worlds* was broadcast, Readick was already one of the most famous voices in radio drama. He appeared in just one film, *Journey into Fear*, starring Orson Welles, who it is said was responsible for most of the direction and casting. Readick died in 1965.

And what about the tiny community of Grover's Mill, New Jersey? Today it still looks pretty much the same as it did when the Martians *didn't* land there in 1938. It's hardly a tourist attraction, although the odd science fiction geek curious about the broadcast still turns up from time to time.

The old wooden water tower still stands, although it is now covered with enough poison ivy to keep Martians or sightseers at a distance. It's an impressive display of endurance considering how, on Halloween night 1938, shotgun-toting Grover's Millers sent splinters flying from the tank, thinking the fog-shrouded tower was a menacing spaceship.

Otherwise, markers of that chaotic night are restricted to one erected by community leaders in 1988 on the fiftieth anniversary of the broadcast: a bronze monument in little Van Nest Park at the edge of Grover's Mill Pond. The 6-foot marker features the bas-relief images of a looming Martian spaceship, Orson Welles at the microphone, and a fear-stricken family huddled around a radio. The inscription claims that *The Mercury Theatre on the Air*'s dubious achievement was 'a landmark in broadcast history, provoking continuing thought about media responsibility, social psychology, and civil defence'.

New Jersey's tourist brochures do not mention Grover's Mill – and if it were up to a lot of the community's residents, they would also just as soon forget about the whole darn thing.

\* \* \*

The Martians attack H. G. Wells' home town, Woking in Surrey. The sculpture was created by artist Michael Condron and was unveiled in the town centre in April 1998. (*Alan Gallop*)

Thanks to Orson Welles and *The Mercury Theatre on the Air*, *The War of the Worlds* still marches on in many different formats – and all of them have been influenced by the 1938 version in one way or another.

By the 1950s, science fiction was everybody's favourite genre on television and at the cinema. A 1953 version of *The War of the Worlds*, produced by George Pal (who had already brought *Destination Moon* and *When Worlds Collide* to the screen), directed by Byron Haskin, starring Gene Barry and bankrolled by Paramount 'in glorious Technicolor', thrilled audiences on both sides of the Atlantic. Trailers told expectant audiences, 'It's coming! The biggest story that could ever happen to our world! Filling the screen with a mighty panorama of earth-shaking fury! This could be the beginning of the end for the human race for what men first thought were meteors or the too-often ridiculed flying saucers are in reality the flaming vanguard of the invasion from Mars! Is there nothing that can stop the Martian death machines?'

Perhaps acknowledging the reaction of the American public following Welles' 1938 radio version, audiences were also told, 'Panic sweeps around the globe as the great masses of mankind flee blindly in a headlong stampede of hysteria! Now, after two years in the making, H. G. Wells' most famous and fantastic story comes to the screen!'

Audiences paying to see the film would, of course, have been expecting a thrilling adventure – unlike those caught unawares by the radio version fifteen years before. It was a good night at the movies.

Stephen Spielberg's 2005 version of *The War of the Worlds* was a different kettle of fish altogether. Starring Tom Cruise and set in America at the start of the twenty-first century, it made George Pal's version look tame. Very real-looking Martian war machines yomped their way across New York, devouring anything and anyone daring to get in their way. H. G. Wells would have been proud of the way Spielberg's writers had clung to the spirit of his original story and yet reheated it for a contemporary audience. It's big and noisy and Welles would probably have enjoyed it if he had lived long enough to see it.

A musical version of *The War of the Worlds*, written by Jeff Wayne, has been playing in large arenas for around thirty years. The show grew out of a double album that has sold over 15 million copies worldwide. The spectacular show includes special CGI effects, including illusions and pyrotechnics, with live singers. A hologram of the late actor Richard Burton speaking excerpts from H. G. Wells' novel is projected onto a 100-foot-wide screen. Of all the versions produced since the 1950s, Wayne's is probably most faithful to Wells' original. It will probably be touring giant stadia in another thirty years' time.

The time is now ripe for someone to produce a version of H. G. Wells' story located in its original time and setting, but backed up by today's cinematic technology. Perhaps it would use the recorded voice of Orson Welles himself – or perhaps Christian MacKay, who played the role of the young Welles so brilliantly in the 2009 film *Me and Orson Welles*. Now that would really be something...

* * *

Many have questioned the nationwide panic caused by Welles' version of *The War of the Worlds*. Was it genuine? Or was it simply a chance for the media to run a fantastic story that would sell newspapers? The answer? It was both.

There is no doubt that many people were scared out of their wits by the play. The screaming headlines and breathless stories about what went on in American cities, towns and small communities is testament to that. But many reporters in the 1930s – and even today – are prone to helping interviewees along when they do not get what they want from their subjects. Thus a question sometimes takes the form of a statement, such as, 'I bet you and your family were surely scared out of your living daylights?' The answer might be 'Yes,' but the quote would then appear as, 'My family and I were sure scared out of our living daylights.' Once the question had been positively answered, answer and question would then be combined into a single 'sensational' quote.

Media reports show that a percentage of the American population were naïve and, in some cases, plain stupid when it came to hearing about Martians landing through a radio programme. A few years before his death, Howard Koch told a television interviewer, 'I was disappointed in the gullibility of the American people who accepted the most outrageous things as truths at that time. There were – still are – a lot of good schools in the United States, but I guess there were some that did not teach the fundamental thing of how to think for yourself. In that aspect, *The War of the Worlds* was a warning.'

There have been other hoaxes over the radio, television and in newspapers since 1938 and occasionally people are taken in and believe what they read, hear or see if it appears genuine – including this author.

A few years ago, I was alone at home watching TV on a wet Saturday afternoon, remote in hand, zapping from one channel to another trying to find something decent to watch. I came across what appeared to be a rolling news programme carrying live reports from London's Heathrow Airport following a terrible plane crash. I immediately sat up and took notice for two reasons: I once worked at Heathrow as a news reporter (and had covered plane crashes there) and I lived relatively near the airport. So why wasn't I hearing wailing sirens from emergency services with depots close to my home?

Eyewitnesses were interviewed along with airport officials, none of whom I recognised. I didn't recognise any news reporters either, but what they were describing was entirely plausible. Great clouds of smoke from the crashed plane were seen on the television, billowing high into the air, and I went out of the house to see if I could see anything coming from the direction of the airport – but saw nothing.

Senior government officials were also interviewed on camera. I had never heard of any of them. Neither had I heard of the airline whose plane had crashed, or the type of aircraft involved in the disaster.

And then the penny dropped. It was 'a dramatic construction' of what might happen if a passenger plane had crashed at Heathrow. The people I had seen on screen were very convincing actors. I had done exactly the same as millions of Americans had done some seventy years before – tuned into a programme that had already started and appeared to be real, and believed everything I had seen and heard. Like those Americans in 1938, I had not switched to other channels to check if they were carrying the same story. I just sat there and believed everything going on in front of me.

As the credits rolled at the end of the programme, it was made clear that we had been watching a fictional documentary. No doubt this was made clear at the beginning, but I'd missed that part.

Would I have been taken in if I had been listening to the radio back in 1938 and heard that aliens had landed in my country? Possibly. Back in the early 1970s my friend Jim Nunn bought me a birthday present of a double LP vinyl record set of the famous broadcast. It had not been commercially available for over thirty years and was now on sale to anyone who wanted to hear it, cleverly packaged in a sleeve that reproduced the lurid headlines used by newspapers across America the day after the show went on air. The interesting sleeve notes by Howard Koch also offered insights into how the programme was created, and comments about working with Orson Welles.

After playing it for the first time, I realised that the radio play still worked. I understood how the public was originally fooled into thinking that a real alien invasion had taken place. The acting is realistic and the terrific sound effects lift the show from a simple play into a thrilling experience, putting listeners on the spot as creatures from another planet attempt to take over our world.

While most of today's public takes tales of UFO sightings with a pinch of salt, over 800 sightings were reported between 1993 and 1996 alone. Both the British and American governments have been taking sightings seriously for years. Hundreds of declassified UFO documents have been released by Britain's National Archives – more than 4,000 pages of material dating back to 1981.

One of the files released in August 2010 reveals that even Winston Churchill was concerned about the effect alien sightings might have on the British public and their morale. The file includes a letter stating that Winston Churchill had ordered a fifty-year cover-up of a wartime sighting made by a reconnaissance plane and its crew returning from a mission over occupied Europe. They spotted an unidentified flying object, 'which hovered noiselessly' over Cumbria. On hearing of the encounter, Churchill is said to have uttered, 'The event should be immediately classified since it would create mass panic amongst the general population and destroy one's belief in the Church.'

Churchill almost certainly knew about the effect *The War of the Worlds* had on the American public a few years before and was anxious to avoid it happening again in England.

After all, it had happened before. It might happen again. It might happen still.

# Howard Koch's
# *The War of the Worlds* Script

The following is five sample pages from Mr Koch's forty-seven-page adaptation of H. G. Wells' *The War of the Worlds* for *The Mercury Theatre on the Air*, broadcast across the United States by the CBS network on Sunday 30 October 1938 at 8 p.m. Eastern Standard Time.

Before handing over the fifty-year-old typewritten script to Sotheby's New York auction house in 1988, Koch added a few words to the cover page, stating, 'This script of my radio play *WAR OF THE WORLDS* was one used in the broadcast …. Corrections made by Orson Welles.' This isn't quite correct as the script – which sold at auction for $143,000 (at over $3,000 per page, probably the most expensive radio script ever written) – was not one actually used by any Mercury actors or CBS technical staff, but a copy handed to Koch on the day before the broadcast went on air, containing annotations by Orson Welles and the CBS censor. Koch was not personally present in the studio when the play was broadcast. While all scripts used by cast and crew were confiscated by police following the broadcast – and never returned – Koch's own version remained safe and sound in his apartment on New York's 72nd Street and he was never asked to return it. Fortunately, Koch had the good sense to take photocopies of each page before putting it up for sale.

On some pages handwritten numbers can be seen in the right-hand margin. These are timings, which were noted down roughly every 10–15 seconds throughout the play's running time to ensure the piece did not overrun its one-hour slot.

ORSON WELLES

We know now that in the early years of the 20th Century ~~that~~ this world was being watched closely by intelligences greater than man's and yet as mortal as hhis own. We know now that as human beings busied themselves about their various concerns they were scrutinized and studied, perhaps almost as narrowly as a man with a microscope might scrutinize the transient creatures that swarm and multiply in a drop of water. With infinite complacence people went to and fro over the earth about their little affairs, serene in the assurance of their dominion over this small spinning fragment of solar driftwood which by chance or design man has inherited out of the dark mystery of Time and Space. Yet across an immense ethereal gulf, minds that are to our minds as ours are to the beasts in the jungle, intellects vast, cool and unsympathetic regarded this earth with envious eyes and slowly and surely drew their plans against us, ~~and~~ In the 39th year of the 20th Century came the great disillusionment.

It was near the end of October. Business was better. The war scare was over. More men were back at work. Sales were picking up. On this particular evening, October 30th, the Crosley service estimated that thirty-two million people were listening in on~~their~~ radios.

---

On page one of the script, a few words have been cut and a comma added, probably to make it easier for Welles to deliver the introduction. It is interesting to note that the script clearly shows that the play was originally to have been set 'in the 39th year of the 30th century'. A handwritten '2' has been added. Reference to the thirtieth century must have been a mistake, as many other references in the play identify a present-day milieu, including locations, music and technology.

-2-

ANNOUNCER ONE:

..... for the next 24 hours not much change in temperature. A
slight atmospheric disturbance of undetermined origin is reported
over Nova Scotia, causing a low pressure area to move down rather
rapidly over the north eastern states, bringing a forecast of
rain, accompanied by winds of light gale force. Maximum
temperature 66 .. minimum 48. [The weather report comes to you
from the ~~United States~~ Government Weather Bureau ~~, Washington, D. C.~~ .].

We now take you to the Meridian Room in the Hotel Park Plaza in
~~in~~ down town New York, where you will be entertained by the music
of Ramon Raquello and his orchestra.

(SPANISH THEME SONG .. FADES)

ANNOUNCER THREE

Good evening, ladies and gentlemen. From the Meridian room in
the Park Plaza in New York City, we bring you the music of
Ramon Raquello and his orchestra. With a touch of the ~~real~~
Spanish, Ramon Raquello leads off with _La Cumparsita_

(PIECE STARTS PLAYING)

ANNOUNCER TWO:

Ladies and gentlemen, we interrupt our program of dance music
to bring you a special bulletin from the Intercontinental Radio
News. At twenty minutes before eight, Central Time, Professor
Farrell of the ~~Yerkes~~ Mount Jennings Observatory, Chicago, Illinois, reports
observing several explosions of incandescent gas, occurring at
regular intervals on the planet Mars.

(MORE)

On page two, evidence of the CBS censor's pencil can be seen, changing references
to 'the United States Weather Bureau, Washington D. C.' to the non-existent
'Government Weather Bureau'. 'Yerkes Observatory, Chicago' has become the
fictional 'Mount Jennings Observatory'. The choice of a piece of tango music known
as 'La Cumparsita' appears to have been a last-minute decision; the title has been
written in a blank space by hand.

-3-

(ANNOUNCER TWO (CONT'D)

The spectroscope indicates the gas to be hydrogen and moving
towards the earth with enormous velocity. Professor Pierson of
the observatory at Princeton ~~University~~ confirms Farrell's
observation, and describes the phenomenon as (quote) like a jet of
blue flame shot from a gun (unquote). We now return you to the
music of Ramon Raquello, playing for you in the Meridian Room
of the Park Plaza Hotel, situated in down town New York.

(MUSIC PLAYS FOR A FEW MOMENTS UNTIL PIECE ENDS ... SOUND OF
APPLAUSE) - CUT TO        *Now a Tune that never loses favor, the ever popular "Star Dust"*   4.45

                ANNOUNCER TWO        *Ramon Raquello and his orchestra*

Ladies and gentlemen, following on the news given in our
bulletin a moment ago, the ~~United States~~ Meterological Bureau has
requested the large observatories of the country to keep an
astronomical watch on any further disturbances occuring on the
planet Mars. Due to the unusual nature of this occurance, we
have arranged an interview with the noted astronomer, Professor
Pierson, who will give us his views on this event. In a few
moments we will take you to the Princeton Observatory ~~situated
on the campus~~ at Princeton, New Jersey. We return you until
then to the music of Ramon Raquello and his orchestra.    5.50

(MUSIC)

                ANNOUNCER TWO

We are now ready to take you to the Princeton Observatory at
Princeton ~~University~~ where ~~Dick~~ Carl Phillips, our commentator, will
interview Professor Richard Pierson, famous astronomer. We take
you now to Princeton, New Jersey.

Page three is full of last-minute changes or additions by both the censor and Welles.
The censor, afraid that the script might be too location-specific, has changed 'Princeton
University' to simply 'Princeton'. Welles has added additional words for an announcer
introducing one of the many musical interludes heard during the early part of the play:
'Now a tune that never loses favor, the ever popular "Star Dust". Ramon Raquello
and his orchestra.' The name of the on-the-spot reporter who will later describe the
scene at Grover's Mill and is annihilated in the process is changed from 'Dick Phillips'
to 'Carl Phillips'.

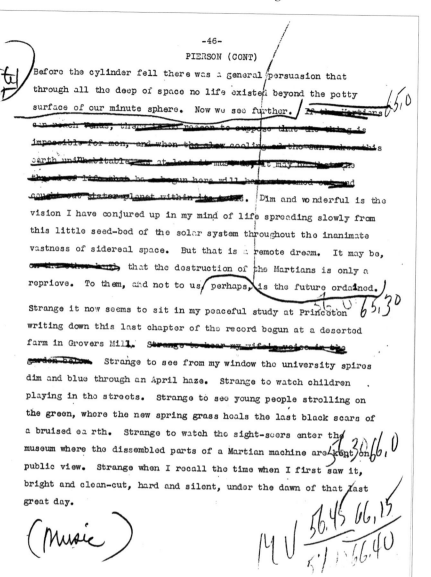

-46-

PIERSON (CONT)

Before the cylinder fell there was a general persuasion that through all the deep of space no life existed beyond the petty surface of our minute sphere. Now we see further. ~~If the Martians can reach Venus, there is no reason to suppose that the thing is impossible for men, and when the slow cooling of the sun makes this earth uninhabitable, as at last it must do, it may be that the thread of life which has begun here will have streamed out and caught our sister planet within its toils.~~ Dim and wonderful is the vision I have conjured up in my mind of life spreading slowly from this little seed-bed of the solar system throughout the inanimate vastness of sidereal space. But that is a remote dream. It may be, ~~on the other hand,~~ that the destruction of the Martians is only a reprieve. To them, and not to us, perhaps, is the future ordained.

Strange it now seems to sit in my peaceful study at Princeton writing down this last chapter of the record begun at a deserted farm in Grovers Mill. ~~Strange to hear my wife's voice in the garden below.~~ Strange to see from my window the university spires dim and blue through an April haze. Strange to watch children playing in the streets. Strange to see young people strolling on the green, where the new spring grass heals the last black scars of a bruised earth. Strange to watch the sight-seers enter the museum where the dissembled parts of a Martian machine are kept on public view. Strange when I recall the time when I first saw it, bright and clean-cut, hard and silent, under the dawn of that last great day.

( Music )

By the time the actors arrived at page forty-six of the script, broadcast time was becoming tight and Welles made more last-minute cuts. Nearly six lines of his own dialogue is removed from his monologue at the end of the play and some sentences are altered in order for them to 'read' better – something quite common in radio drama. At the bottom of the page the running time is clearly shown as fifty-six minutes and forty-five seconds – leaving just enough time for Welles to conclude the play with an explanation.

— 47 —

/Ladies and gentlemen, this is Orson Welles. / out of character to)

I assure you that the WAR OF THE WORLDS has no further significance than as the holiday offering it was intended to be. The
Mercury Theatre's own Radio version of dressing up in a sheet and
jumping out of a bush and saying Boo! Starting now, we couldn't
soap all your windows and steal all your garden gates, by tomorrow
night,.. so we did the next best thing. We annihilated the world
before your very ears, and utterly destroyed the (CBS Columbia Broadcasting
System.) You will be relieved, I hope, to learn that we didn't
mean it, and that both institutions are still open for business.
So good-bye everybody, and remember, please, for the next
day or so, the terrible lesson you learned tonight. That grinning,
glowing, globular invader of your living-room is an inhabitant
of the pumpkin patch, and if your doorbell rings and nobody's
there, that was no Martian .. it's Hallowe'en.

(Music)

67.30
58

Welles has made an important addition to the script's final page – page forty-seven – by writing in a an extra line to reassure the audience that the play is now over and that he is only an actor and is stepping out of character to deliver a final message. It begins, 'Ladies and gentlemen, this is Orson Welles, out of character to assure you that the *WAR OF THE WORLDS* has no further significance than the holiday offering it was intended to be.' By the time he delivers his final line ('… and if your doorbell rings and nobody's there, that was no Martian … it's Hallowe'en.') the play had run for fifty-eight minutes, leaving time for Bernard Herrmann to conduct the closing piece of music and for announcer Dan Seymour to tell listeners what they will hear at the same time the following Sunday.

# Bibliography and Sources

## Books

*The Fabulous Century: 1930–1940* (Time-Life Books, 1969).

Bogdanovich, Peter, *This Is Orson Welles* (Da Capo Press, 1998).

Brown, Robert J., *Manipulating the Ether: The Power of Broadcast Radio in Thirties America* (McFarland & Co., 1998).

Callow, Simon, *Orson Welles – The Road to Xanadu* (Jonathan Cape, 1995).

Callow, Simon, *Orson Welles – Hello Americans* (Jonathan Cape, 2006).

Cantril, Hadley, *The Invasion from Mars* (Princeton University Press, 1940).

Estrin, Mark (ed.), *Orson Welles: Interviews* (University Press of Mississippi, 2002).

Houseman, John, *Unfinished Business* (Chatto & Windus, 1986).

Koch, Howard, *The War of the Worlds*, the original 1938 script written for *The Mercury Theatre on the Air* (unpublished).

Koch, Howard, *The Panic Broadcast* (Avon Books, 1971).

Levine, Justin, *History & Analysis of the Federal Communication Commission's Response to Radio Broadcast Hoaxes* (Law School of Los Angeles, 1999).

Parrinder, Patrick & Partington, John S., *The Reception of H. G. Wells in Europe* (London: Thoemmes Continuum, 2005).

Smith, Sally Bedell, *In All His Glory: The Life of William S. Paley* (Simon & Schuster, 1990).

Wells, H. G., *The War of the Worlds* (Heinemann, 1898).

## Newspapers, Magazines and Comics

*Daily News*, (New York: 31 October 1938).

*Manchester Guardian* (1 November 1938).

*Harper's Magazine*, 'The Men from Mars' by John Houseman (December 1948).

*Los Angeles Herald Express* (10 November 1938).

*New York Daily News* (31 October 1938).

*The New York Times* (30, 31 October 1938; 1, 2, 3, 6 November 1938; 21 October 1988; 18 August 1995).

*New York Tribune* (2 November 1938).

*New York World Telegram* (1, 2 November 1938).

*Orlando Sentinel* (30 October 1988).

*Radio Digest* (February 1939).

*Radio Guide* (November 1938).

*Saturday Evening Post* (3 February 1940).

*St. Louis Globe-Democrat* (31 October 1938).

*Superman #62: Black Magic on Mars* (DC Comics, January/February 1950).

*Time* (9 May 1938, 7 November 1938, 16 March 2010).

*Trenton Evening Times* (31 October 1938, 1 November 1938).

*Trenton State Gazette* (1 November 1938).

# Radio and Television Broadcasts

Interview with Orson Welles and H. G. Wells (San Antonio, Texas: Radio KTSA, 29 October 1940).

*Arena – The Orson Welles Story*, Welles' interview with Leslie Megahey (BBC, May 1982).

*The Dean Martin Show*, Orson Welles talks about *The War of the Worlds* (NBC, 1970).

*The Merv Griffin Show*, interview with Orson Welles (20 October 1985).

*Monitor*, Orson Welles' interview with Huw Weldon (BBC, 1960).

*The Orson Welles Sketchbook*, Episode 5, 'The Martian Invasion' (BBC, 21 May 1955).

# Online

The British Library's newspaper collection, *http://catalogue.bl.uk*.

The Bernard Herrmann Estate, *www.thebernardherrmannestate.com*.

The Bernard Herrmann Society, *www.bernardherrmann.org*.

Critical Past, *www.criticalpast.com*.

Wellesnet (the Orson Welles web resource), *www.wellesnet.com*.

# Other

The Library of Congress, Washington, DC.

The National Archives and Records Administration (especially Lee Ann Potter, education specialist), College Park, Maryland.

# Acknowledgements

My sincere thanks to a small but select group of people who were kind enough to supply me with information used in this book, sound advice that will (I hope) keep me out of trouble, or inspiration through their own writings.

Thanks, then, to:

Peter Koch of Woodstock, New York
Norman Rudman of MCN, Elk, California
Peter Wise of Cranbury, New Jersey
Paul Heyer of Wilfred Laurier University, Waterloo, Ontario
Bill McMahon of Metropolitan Washington Old Time Radio Club and Radio Recall
Frank Passage of Verona, New Jersey
Martin Grams of Delta, Pennsylvania

... and to my enthusiastic editor Thom Hutchinson at Amberley Publishing, who demonstrated his excitement and passion for this project right from the word go. If only all editors... but let's stop there.